Coping With Loss

Nurturing Resilience Through Grief and Difficult Times, a Practical Toolkit for Self-Help Healing

Maria Holden

Table of Contents

Introduction

You don't go around grieving all the time, but the grief is still there and always will be. –Nigella Lawson

Just a while back, I read the true story of Norma and Gordon Yeager (Penrose, 2021), who got married on the day Norma graduated high school in 1939. Married for 72 years, the couple traveled and raised their two kids together. To say that they were inseparable would be an understatement. They operated the family business and participated in the same clubs, just to be beside one another for almost the entirety of their lives.

They were fortunate to have left the world together. After being injured in a car accident, the couple was admitted to a hospital, where they kept asking about each other's condition so much that even the staff decided that it was time for them to be shifted into the same room. Eyewitnesses, including hospital staff and relatives, swear that even after Gordon breathed his last, his heart kept beating for an hour or more on the monitor. It wasn't until Norma stopped responding that his heart finally stopped beating. It seemed almost as if he was waiting for her to enter the afterlife together as well! In a last touching tribute to their everlasting love, their daughter and other family members decided to lay them in a single casket, holding hands, for their funeral.

Not everyone is as lucky in a loss. Most of us struggle through feelings of loneliness and despair, wondering how we will ever manage to extricate ourselves from the grip of these powerful emotions. We often equate loss with the death of a loved one. However, this need not always be the case.

Today, we are aware that loss can stem from losing a pet, moving cities, changing houses, losing or resigning from a job you loved, or any other major life change. In short, it is natural to mourn a person, a place, or even a state of being. For instance, have we not thought back with regret upon the lost innocence of our childhoods, even if we haven't faced any deep-seated trauma as such?

The following are some losses that could result in feelings of grief:

The loss of a beloved person—a friend, spouse, family member, or even a pet—can be devastating for many. This physical absence of a much-beloved companion with whom you used to spend quality time can affect you emotionally, and until you get into a new routine, it might seem that a part of your life has ended too.

The end of a relationship—professional or personal—such as divorce, breakup, changing jobs, etc. can be heartbreaking. You might have made plans, and your dreams could have been wound up with the relationships you were forging. When they end, it suddenly seems exhausting to have to rebuild them again from scratch. Moving to a new city or house can likewise make you intensely miss environments that are cozy and comfortable. You might feel out of place until you find your footing.

Lack of financial stability is a loss that not many people open up about. Yet, it can leave you just as vulnerable as any other loss. You feel that you haven't done enough or that your life should have been better than it is. The shattering of long-held dreams or goals that didn't work out can also leave you feeling empty and hollow. Such scenarios often leave you grappling with the question, "What next?"

Ill health can similarly make you feel alone. The loss of your health can seem gutting. You may also be filled with regret that you did not do more when you were well. Similarly, aging and the loss of youth can affect many people with a longing for the past. With the sometimes unrealistic beauty standards that are promoted in the media today, women feel the edge of this most. Infertility or miscarriages are another very common loss that many women or parents silently carry around. The fact that there wasn't a "visible" baby present doesn't mitigate the grief that comes with such a loss.

Healing from loss and the grief associated with it is a complicated process that people often brush aside as something to be "faced" or "dealt with." The inability to take grief and loss in one's stride is, likewise, considered "shameful" or a "weakness" that one has to somehow weed out from their system. In practice, this is easier said than done. The reality is that one may not "overcome" grief entirely. With time, it will definitely get less painful, and with practice, you can learn to adjust to it as a part of your life. Thus, the term that we are looking at is "coping" rather than the more unrealistic "overcoming."

Seeing as how grief can emanate from a variety of sources, let us now look at what it can do to a person. As we have discussed, people experience grief in many ways—physically, mentally, and emotionally. Thus, when people say that they feel the "pain" of grief, they aren't exaggerating. It isn't unusual for grief to manifest itself as bodily pains, aches, restlessness, or intense fatigue. You may feel a cocktail of confusing emotions such as relief, regret, guilt, and sadness. Mentally, you may feel: An inability to focus on things, being ill-equipped to make decisions, or difficulties in keeping track of things. Since grief is bound up with stress, in the long run, a person unable to manage their grief may face symptoms of deteriorating health, including lowered immunity. This can lead to physical ailments, including chronic diseases, as well as mental health issues.

It is essential to remember that loss affects each individual differently and that there is no "right" way of grieving. To some people, your loss may seem inconsequential, while theirs may seem trivial to you. Kindness and patience are the two key ingredients in not just coping with your own loss but also in dealing with others who are grieving.

In my experience, if there is one important factor that helps people surmount grief, it is "resilience." Technically, this word means to "bounce back" after challenges, setbacks, or failures. Think of a stress ball that you squeeze with the full force of your palm. Let go of it, and it will retain its original shape. This is an example of resilience in an inanimate object. As far as people are concerned, loss can not leave us totally unscathed. Think now of a sheet of paper that has been crumpled. Flatten it out again, and you will find that, despite the creases, the paper can still be used for writing. This is probably a more accurate description of how we emerge from grief.

The word resilience should bring hope to our minds. This is because resilience is far from a "gift" that only a few people are endowed with. Instead, it is a quality that anyone can develop over time with practice. In other words, like a muscle that can be trained to be stronger and fitter, you can grow your resilience to develop better immunity against your grief. This does not mean that you refuse to acknowledge or that you ignore your grief. Rather, you embrace your grieving process and channel it so that you can emerge stronger for having undergone it—like a rite of passage.

Coping With Loss: Nurturing Resilience Through Grief and Difficult Times, A Practical Toolkit for Self-Help Healing is the ideal resource for anyone who wants to navigate loss and grief in their personal or professional lives. It combines actionable steps on managing grief, expert opinions, and personal anecdotes of people who have successfully handled their grief.

The sections of this book have been arranged to cover a scientific and medical understanding of how grief works and to finally help your readers become pillars of support for others who are grieving. The following is a brief glimpse of what this book offers:

- In Chapter 1, we try to understand grief and its manifestations. We will also explore the types of grief as well as the different stages that a grieving person might go through.

- Chapter 2 will allow us to bust some long-standing myths that we have heard about loss and grief. This will, in turn, help you realize that what you feel is not just normal but also experienced by others like you.

- In Chapter 3, we look at how to cope with the emotional turmoil associated with grief. This includes self-care practices such as a healthy expression of your emotions and the support of personal and professional help whenever necessary.

- Chapter 4 builds on the previous chapter to explore tools and techniques for inner healing. We look at some methods that will help you channel and pour out your self-expression in productive, meaningful, and creative ways.

- In Chapter 5, we look at why honoring yourself and the memory of your loss is a vital part of self-healing. Taking a closer look at some of the barriers that hold back grief, we will look at means of letting grief go.

- Chapter 6 is where we will discuss resilience building. As we have seen, resilience is the power and strength that we derive from suffering and grief. Here, we discover why emotional and mental resilience can help you recover from loss better.

- In Chapter 7, we look at the "what next" of this journey as we move forward and make meaning of our stories. This stage will help you find a purpose in your life.

In the last culminating section of this book, Chapter 8, we address the question of how our experience can be turned into a powerful tool with which to help others in their grieving journey.

I sincerely hope that *Coping With Loss* will guide you to reflect on your own experience(s) with loss and the challenges you have faced. Further, the extensive toolkit that accompanies the book will encourage you to tap into your self-help healing process.

As a last word, before we dive into the beautiful world of transcending grief, I would only like each of you to start asking yourselves why you have embarked on this journey toward healing and rediscovery of yourselves.

Chapter 1:

Understanding Grief

It takes strength to make your way through grief, to grab hold of life and let it pull you forward. –Patti Davis

One of the greatest challenges in dealing with grief is that not everyone understands what it is like. It is like the oft-quoted parable of the six blind men trying to define the appearance of an elephant by touching it. It is not always easy to label and reduce the healing process into common, understandable patterns because people experience grief in different ways. A blogger named Monica, who lost her father, describes how she continued to miss him even five years after his passing from brain cancer in a personal story (Monica, 2020). She thought of him every single day and would often reminisce over how he would have loved a particular movie she watched and so on. Every memory of hers after him almost seemed like an injustice because he couldn't experience it. When her father passed away, she was only 23, a time when she had just entered adulthood, which probably affected her even more. She goes on to explain exactly the point we made earlier—that grief is a very personal and subjective experience and that your journey toward rediscovering your life should not be based on other people's experiences.

To have a brief understanding of how grief works, it is always good to have textbook knowledge of it. This is what we will attempt to do in this chapter. As I keep reiterating, these are not the be-all and end-all of how it operates, but understanding grief from a psychological perspective might help you in your personal journey toward identifying some aspects of your battle with it, at least.

Let us start with the classic types of grief that are usually recognized and discussed from a medical standpoint.

Types of Grief

As grief is associated with particular losses and situations that people go through, it is indeed hard for us to arrive at a consensus regarding all the different possible ways in which it may manifest. However, one of the first attempts at breaking down the complexity of grief has been in trying to categorize it. None of us may wholly agree with such a water-tight compartmentalization. Still, as you read through the following descriptions, it may bring to mind certain qualities of your own experiences and help you make better sense of it. At this stage, we are only attempting to understand it better.

The following are some types of grief (*What is grief?*, 2023; Smith et al., 2019):

Abbreviated Grief

When you know that a loss is around the corner, you can start your grieving process early without even consciously being aware of it. This is the case with an ailing loved one, for instance. You may perhaps already know that they won't survive, and you spend each day in the knowledge that this may be the last day with them. When the actual loss happens, the overwhelm of the moment is sometimes replaced quickly with a sense of relief and regret. This may seem confusing, and people often end up beating themselves up for having gotten over it "so fast" or for having "forgotten" their loved one quickly. However, the truth is that you were already grieving for them while they were still alive. This "fast" healing is as normal as the prolonged grieving that we expect because people are ultimately on different timelines with grief.

Anticipatory Grief

As we already mentioned, beginning to process grief before the actual loss has happened can sometimes be beneficial in the healing process. At the same time, it may also leave you feeling very tired and exhausted, even as you are handling your emotions. Anticipatory grief could help you face the loss better. However, it is important to keep in mind not to get distracted from spending your last moments with the person, place, or situation that will no longer be a part of your life.

Collective Grief

We think of grief as something that happens to us. And yet, with incidents such as wars, natural disasters, genocide, or a pandemic, often the grief is not just your own but that of the entire community that you are a part of. Suddenly, there is a "new normal" for our society that everyone in it is coming to terms with. In such times, collective grief can be both a blessing and a curse. On the one hand, it will help you feel less alone in your loss, while at the same time, you could feel overwhelmed by the magnitude of what has happened and how it has impacted the lives of so many. However, there is also hope in imagining a changed and better environment.

Cumulative Grief

Just when we thought that grief could be associated with a single event, it turns out that it may not be as simple as that. When we grieve something, we also think back to every other loss that we have faced before this. For instance, when you mourn the end of a relationship, it may also be the many other broken relationships that you are grieving. This is the cumulative nature of loss. Another instance of this is if you work in a profession such as medicine, law enforcement, or social work that puts you in daily contact with death. After a while, you may feel overwhelmed by each loss you witness. This kind of grief can sometimes add up to magnify your grief disproportionately to the immediate trigger right now.

Delayed Grief

We have often seen and read stories of people who go into shock after a tremendous loss. Some lose their ability to speak or repress the memories that caused the grief. Delayed grief is when you can't grieve right after the loss. It comes back after days, weeks, months, or, in some cases, even after years. The responsibilities of a person after their loss, such as the smooth conduct of a funeral or wrapping up other matters, can also delay their grieving process. One may feel like putting off the mourning until these duties are taken care of. When grief comes back later, the intensity of it can take you by surprise as well.

Inhibited Grief

We touched on this briefly when we talked of grief that does not find a proper outlet. When you lose something or someone you haven't acknowledged in public, you can't mourn their loss to the full extent that you want to. For instance, think of a secret romance that leads to a breakup. It is not just the person you are grieving but also your inability to express anything about it to your near and dear ones. You end up repressing your emotions. It isn't always as conscious of a choice as this, either. Repression is often a subconscious tactic of our mind to handle loss and keep us functioning in the wake of grief. Yet, this dammed-up grief can flow over in the form of physical ailments, panic attacks, insomnia, etc. Inhibited grief can be a very dangerous form of grief, especially when it goes unnoticed and untreated.

Now that we know the types of grief, we will try to explore the symptoms of grief in greater detail in the next section.

Symptoms of Grief

In the introduction to this book, we briefly touched upon how the symptoms of grief can both be varied as well as affect individuals in different ways. Here, we shall try to delve into some of the common ways in which grief can show itself. To do this, generally, we group the symptoms into four main categories: physical, cognitive, behavioral, and emotional (*What is grief?*, 2023; Smith et al., 2019).

Physical Symptoms

As we discussed, the pain of grief can take on a physical form. Of course, it would take a perceptive doctor to recognize that your physical symptoms might be linked to your psychological loss. In many cases, both the physician and the patient miss this vital link and merely end up treating the bodily discomfort without addressing the mental anguish and pain of the patient. So, what could these symptoms look like?

The following list, though not comprehensive, should give you a better idea of what grief can do to your body:

- Headaches

- Crying spells

- Nausea

- Tightness in your throat or chest

- Increased or reduced appetite

- Stomach upset

- Faster heart rate or palpitations

- Muscle, joint, or body pains

- Sleeping too much or too little

- Exhaustion

- Restlessness

As you can see, nobody would think to link the symptoms listed above to grief in particular, and yet they have come up time and again in clinical studies on loss and grief. Chronic grief can take a toll on your health and make your immune system vulnerable, leaving your body more susceptible to infections and diseases.

Cognitive Symptoms

Grief can often leave you feeling mentally "foggy." This could result in poor decisions, the inability to make sound judgments, etc. Here are a few mental symptoms of grief.

- Confusion

- Forgetfulness

- Hyper-vigilance or the inability to let down your guard

- Intrusive memories that leave you dysfunctional at times

- Recurrent thoughts

- Lack of focus or direction

The above can also make you feel mentally exhausted and unable to cope with the nitty-gritty of daily life.

Emotional Symptoms

These are the emotional reactions that intense and protracted grief may bring about. Again, not everyone may show all of these, but some of you may be able to recognize certain components of the traits below in yourselves.

- Denial or trying to hide your real feelings in an attempt to make things seem "normal."

- Anger management issues and directing your anger at others, a divine force, or even yourself over small things.

- Emotional detachment from people and things.

- Depression and feelings of sadness that persist or intensify with time.

- Anxiety and vulnerability over the future.

- Feeling irritated with people and situations.

- Fear and apprehension about everything.

- Guilt at feeling a sense of relief that a relationship is over or that you no longer have to care for a sick person.

- Feeling hopeless and lost.

The emotional impact of grief can be difficult to overcome and could take time and effort.

Behavioral Symptoms

Changes in behavior among those who grieve are very common. As you can imagine, it would take a lot of effort for someone to present a veneer of normalcy when they are trying to cope with loss. The following are some ways in which grief can change people:

- Frequent emotional outbursts of anger or tears

- Increase in conflicts with other people

- Withdrawal from people or avoidance of places that trigger sad memories

- Decrease in performance at work

- Reduced interest in hobbies or pastimes earlier enjoyed

- Substance or alcohol consumption leads to addiction in severe cases

Behavioral changes can be easier to catch, but because not everyone exhibits them, it may take longer for an onlooker to identify the signs of grief in that person.

In the next section, we look at how complications in grief can affect individuals.

Complications in Grief and Prolonged Grief

All grief is complex and can lead to emotional and health problems. However, sometimes grief can grow its roots so deep into a person that weeding it out becomes extremely difficult. Complicated or prolonged grief (*What is grief?*, 2023) can come with its own issues and can disrupt life in many ways. Some things that can lead to and feed off complicated grief include the following:

- **Absent grief**: Not everybody who doesn't show symptoms of grieving is immune to it. Some people are either working through the shock of their loss or trying to process the complex emotions that their grief has left. The lack of outward symptoms can sometimes be more dangerous than an emotional outburst. To understand this better, think of a pressure cooker that does not have a safety valve to let out steam. When the pressure gets too much for the vessel, it could burst, spilling the contents everywhere.

- **Ambiguous loss**: We are mentally and emotionally trained to seek closure even in difficult situations. When that closure is unavailable to us, we often find it hard to process the resulting feelings and thoughts. For instance, the family of a man presumed dead but whose body has not been recovered may suffer more emotionally than if his remains were to be found. Similarly, caring for a loved one who is emotionally inaccessible to us owing to diseases such as dementia or Alzheimer's can cause severe grief without a sense of finality.

- **Disenfranchised grief**: When you grieve but are told that your grief doesn't count, that it is trivial, or that it is abnormal, it can add to the sense of emptiness and vulnerability that you feel. For instance, grieving over the loss of a pet is often dismissed, or the loss of a same-sex partner is invalidated as perverted or criminal in some societies. Because no one around you ever acknowledges your disenfranchised grief, it is haunting.

- **Traumatic grief**: Loss owing to catastrophes, accidents, or violence can sometimes cause a disorder called post-traumatic stress disorder (PTSD). This includes not just grief but also all the symptoms of physical, emotional, or mental trauma. To heal from this form of grief, a person would require clinical help and support. In such cases, licensed professionals may prescribe psychological therapy and, occasionally, medication.

- **Broken heart syndrome**: While grief doesn't kill, it can make living life so stressful that your body keeps releasing stress hormones long after the shock of the loss should have worn off. Stress hormones can cause your heart to beat irregularly and cause it to pump harder. This can, in turn, lead to chest pains similar to those experienced when one experiences a heart attack, giving rise to the name "broken heart" syndrome. Research suggests that women are more prone to this particular form of grief, and though recovery is possible, it could take some time and counseling to get there (Sreenivas, 2021).

So, how do you understand whether grief is prolonged or not? The following could be a few clues that may point in the direction of complicated grief if you feel them a year or more after your loss:

- Feeling like you are dead or that a part of you has died.

- Thoughts of ending your life.

- Inability to accept the loss and deny it altogether.

- Avoidance of reminders about the loss.

- Intense pain (physical, emotional, cognitive, or behavioral) that makes it difficult for you to live a normal life.

- Emotional numbness is the inability to partake in life with all your faculties intact.

- Extreme loneliness and incapacity to be with friends, participate in hobbies or make decisions about the future.

- Slow speech or movements or generally feeling dysfunctional all or most of the time.

- Seeing or hearing things that aren't real.

A word of caution: Do not assume that you are undergoing complicated grief just by the above symptoms alone. If in doubt, it is better to consult a certified therapist who can diagnose the root of your specific problem.

Some of the details that we have discussed in this chapter could seem overwhelming to you, depending on where you stand. You might probably be wondering right now whether the knowledge of all this information will help you at all. However, a thorough understanding of your problem is always the first step to curing it. This is true not just of any ailment but of grief as well.

How Long Does Grief Last "Normally"?

The above is a natural question you will have asked yourself, especially if you have been feeling low over your loss for quite some time now. The fact is that there is no real answer to this question. Grief is something that everyone has to work through. It lasts longer for some, while others seem to move on faster. As already mentioned, just because somebody does not show it outwardly, it does not necessarily mean that they have moved past their grief. At the end of the day, each person is different, and their ways of coping are too. There is no right or wrong way to grieve.

As per the American Psychological Association, grief over a specific loss can last for any duration, between six months and two years (*What is grief?*, 2023). Having said that, one should also remember that grief does not vanish with the waving of a magic wand. Experiencing loss can alter you as a person forever. This is not to scare you, but a gentle reminder that grief can eventually mold you into a stronger person who can withstand more of the disappointments that life will throw your way. Just as metals become stronger after having passed through fire, we become tougher after experiencing loss and grief.

All this is to say that there is no "normal" as far as grief is concerned. What you go through is just as valid as what another may experience. Though you can use all the information in this section to frame a reference point for your feelings, there is no need to feel anxious if your encounter with loss and grief has not tallied exactly with the scientific findings in the area.

Key Takeaways

In our attempt to comprehend grief, we talked about some of its main aspects:

- Grief is not a single entity but can encompass a variety of types born of different kinds of losses. Though we explored the common types of grief discussed in psychology, the truth is that you may experience a combination of them.

- The symptoms of grief can affect you mentally, physically, emotionally, and behaviorally.

- Prolonged or complicated grief can grow from neglecting or ignoring your grief. It can also be the result of specific situations in which certain obstacles have prevented you from grieving fully.

- Lastly, though clinical definitions of how long grief should last generally exist, they only provide a reference. There are no hard-and-fast rules for how long you should or shouldn't grieve.

In the next chapter, we look at some common myths associated with the grieving process and how these may hinder you from self-healing. We also look at the five stages of the process to better understand it.

Chapter 2:

Stages of Grief and Some Myths

About Grieving

*We bereaved are not alone. We belong to the largest company in all the world —
the company of those who have known suffering.* –Helen Keller

In a recent blog article, I came across the beautifully poignant story of
Jelena, who was mourning the loss of her best friend and her
grandmother, both of whom passed within a short span of time. She
says how she felt empty for a while after their deaths. Unhesitatingly,
she shares with us how she would go to her therapist and cry her heart
out for two whole years, unable to talk about what was bothering her.
Despite the fact that she appeared to be in good health, her losses had
shattered her mind. One of her greatest regrets was how she ought to
have done things differently or spent more time with the people who
mattered so much to her. Out walking by a river near her house, she
happened to meet an old woman who finally broke through the gloom
and spoke to her grief. The pearls of wisdom imparted to her by the
woman changed her life.

This was what she told her (*Dealing with grief*, n.d.):

I can feel your pain, it's all over your face. What you need is to focus
on your life passing by your side, you can not be passive, but you have
to grab your life by the horns and actively participate, or you'll be sorry.
Don't let your grief control your life, when you have the power of
healing yourself.

Jelena finally understood something profound—something that even
journaling her grief and therapy had not offered her yet. She finally
recognized that, without her volition and action, it may be impossible

for her to snap out of her negative thoughts. She realized that though she could not change her situation and bring back the people she had lost, she could change the way she viewed her loss.

Often, when we say that time heals wounds, it takes away a sense of our agency in the process. Erroneously, we believe that we will heal automatically over a period of time. However, what we actually need to say to correct this misconception is that, over time, *we* have the power to heal ourselves.

In this chapter, we look at common myths that may impede the process of self-healing. We also look at the five stages of healing from grief and why this theory has both its pluses and negatives.

The Five Stages of Healing

First and foremost, even before we dive into this theory, it is important to keep in mind that grief is more like a roller coaster of ups and downs. There will be days when you feel better or more at ease with yourself, and there will be others when you feel pained, numb, or just emotionally unstable. Even though we call these *the stages of healing*, this process may not work as hierarchically or linearly as one would imagine. There may be times when you feel like you are *regressing* into a previous stage or that there is no real pattern that you can trace in your recovery. There is no need to panic in either of these cases. The following is merely a rough blueprint of what your path should look like. Even if the reality is different, knowing this theory can perhaps bring some solace.

Elisabeth Kübler-Ross, who worked primarily with terminally ill patients coming to terms with their deaths, introduced "The Stages of Grief" in 1969 (Cruse, n.d.). Her theory was later extended to apply to other kinds of loss and grief. The following were what she proposed:

- **Denial:** "No, I won't believe that this is happening to me." At this stage, people refuse to believe that the loss has taken place at all. This is when some go through numbness and shock. For a while, this phase allows the grieving person to let in only as much as they can take. For most people, this phase will be broken when they acknowledge the situation and realize what has happened. Other emotions like sadness, anger, regret, or guilt will take the place of denial once one starts to ask questions.

- **Anger**: "Why me of all people?" Denial gives way to anger. One may feel angry with the universe for letting this happen. Sometimes anger is directed at yourself, and you think that you could have prevented the situation by making different choices. Anger can also be directed at people you feel were responsible for the loss. What you need to remember is that this anger is laced with the pain of loss. Feeling this anger can also be a coping mechanism that delays the pain of abandonment or the meaninglessness of life.

- **Bargaining**: "Please take away this loss, and in return, I promise to live a better life." For some, the preoccupation with what could have been becomes an obsession. They keep thinking of ways in which their loss could have been averted. They feel that their actions were directly or indirectly responsible for the loss, and they keep thinking back to the day, trying to imagine a different outcome. This can lead to feelings of severe guilt. However, this stage is also one where the individual is negotiating with the grief of loss.

- **Depression**: "I feel so sad and lonely because of my loss." Once a person realizes the extent of their loss, the depressive symptoms kick in. This might include a loss of sleep or appetite and frequent crying spells. Other common accompanying feelings could be loneliness, self-pity, and emptiness. Low energy and a lack of enjoyment in activities you once loved to characterize this phase. Since depression could set in a little later after the loss, many consider it abnormal and something to be snapped out of. However, this is when the real mourning takes place, and as such, it plays an important role in the healing process.

- **Acceptance**: "I have lost something or somebody valuable, but I am at peace with it." The resolution of all the negative emotions associated with grieving eventually leads to an embrace of your loss. This doesn't always mean that you have moved past your grief or that you are no longer affected by it. On the contrary, there may still be days when you cry or feel low. However, you will learn to cope with it and continue with life. Acceptance can be hard when you don't want things to change. But with time, one might learn to have more good days than bad ones and slowly learn to forge new memories and relationships.

Above all else, it is important to be kind and patient with yourself throughout this journey. Only you know what you are undergoing, and thus, let other people's expectations not become your benchmark for your healing and recovery.

Myths and Facts About Grieving

There are many myths associated with the grieving process that can be terrible for a person who needs to go through it. It sets up stereotypes of either excessive or not enough sadness for the loss that one has encountered. In addition to one's loss, this can be extremely hard to face.

This section will look at some common myths about grief and set them against a more accurate picture of what it might look like for you.

Myth #1: The pain will decrease sooner if you ignore it.

Fact: Bottling up your pain will not make it go away. In fact, it will make you feel more miserable inside. It is always wiser to learn how to cope with the pain of loss and to let it out gently.

Myth #2: One must be strong while grieving.

Fact: Crying is a normal reaction to loss, and so is being afraid, sad, or vulnerable. You are helping yourself and your family more by showing your true self rather than hiding it.

Myth #3: Not crying means that you aren't grieving enough.

Fact: People react in different ways to grief. There isn't a particular amount of crying that you should or shouldn't do. Those who don't cry may express their sadness differently. That is normal, too.

Myth #4: Grief lasts for around a year.

Fact: There isn't a timeframe for grief. It is person- and context-specific.

Myth #5: Moving on means forgetting your grief or the person you have lost.

Fact: Moving on is a natural process of life. One can't let loss stop your life. That does not mean that you have forgotten what you have lost. It means that you have adjusted to the new life. The memories of the person or thing you lost will forever be a part of you.

Myth #6: Grief ends at some point.

Fact: Grief does not end. It will become a part of who you become. We learn to adjust to it, manage it, and live our lives. There are moments in life when you will still feel sad. That is all right, as long as it is not stopping you from living your life.

Myth #7: Your life will become normal again after grieving.

Fact: Your life will always remain changed owing to your loss. But that need not be a bad thing. You will learn to adapt to a new normal and continue with your life in the best possible manner.

Myth #8: Grief reduces a little at a time until you recover from it.

Fact: Experiencing grief is more akin to a roller-coaster ride of ups and downs. There will be enjoyable days and weeks, then those that make you unhappy. You may feel that you have "overcome" it, but an incident or memory might again leave you teary-eyed. There is no straight line where grief is concerned.

Myth #9: If you display photos or don't get rid of the belongings of the person you have lost, it means that you are stuck.

Fact: How you want to remember your loved one is totally up to you. If you want to give away their belongings, that is fine. Keeping the items only means that you want to keep their memory alive. This does not have a direct bearing on whether you have healed or not.

Myth #10: You need to conduct a funeral to gain closure over the loss of a loved one.

Fact: Some people may perhaps want a traditional funeral for the ones they love. However, this need not make grieving any less of a harder or faster process than it is.

Myth #11: You have to find meaning and closure to get over your grief.

Fact: This statement is riddled with problems because, firstly, you can't aim to "get over" your grief. Secondly, as with life, there is sometimes no meaning or closure to grief, except for the ones that you give to it. In fact, meaning-making itself is a personal process. Not everyone will assign the same meaning or importance to an event.

Myth #12: Certain losses are easier to cope with than others.

Fact: A person who loses a pet cat may, at times, grieve more over the loss than another who loses a family member they weren't very close with. You can't judge whose loss is greater or lesser. Only the person who has experienced the loss is aware of it.

Myth #13: Children don't grieve, or they get over it faster.

Fact: Children are capable of grieving just as much as grownups. Even children have to work through their feelings of grief to cope with it. Just because they are younger doesn't mean they can effortlessly and automatically overcome their loss and sadness over it. However, because children learn and adapt faster than adults, it could be true that they are more resilient.

Myth #14: A miscarriage is easier to bear. After all, the parents did not actually see the child.

Fact: For expecting mothers or parents, the child they carry is as real as a child who is born. Thus, expecting these parents to get over the loss of a child who never made it into the world is unreasonable and cruel.

Myth #15: Having another child after the loss of one can help reduce the grief.

Fact: You can't replace your love for one child with another. Having a child merely to cope with the loss of one may make you less present for your next child. These matters are always personal choices that parents have to discuss and plan.

Myth #16: Journaling or art therapy helps with loss.

Fact: It might help when the person grieving can express themselves better in words or in certain arts. However, not everyone finds writing cathartic or enjoyable. Even good writers may not always find writing about their grief healing. Finally, it boils down to whether it works for you or not.

Myth #17: The tactics you use for grieving must help others too.

Fact: Every person has different ways of handling grief. Some techniques might help some people more than others. Ultimately, each one has to identify and decide on methods that help them.

Myth #18: Support groups or therapy are always effective.

Fact: Talking about grief can be a powerful method of expressing and dealing with it. However, therapy and support groups are not for everyone. Some people don't want to talk publicly about their loss or may not be able to bond with the therapist. They will find other ways of soothing themselves.

Myth #19: after losing a partner or spouse, you need to date again in _ number of years. Otherwise, it means you are stuck.

Fact: Some choose to date again and to give love a chance. Some are at peace where they are in life, or they aren't in a hurry to move into a relationship again. Both ways are normal ways to move on with one's life.

Myth #20: If your loss is real, you will find the continued presence of the person in your life.

Fact: As comforting as this may sound, you need not always find the presence of your dearly departed throughout your life. You may remember them at times, and with time, their memory might begin to fade. As long as you are at peace with it, there is no one way to heal yourself.

Myth #21: If you have faith in God, grieving becomes easier, or God will not give you more than you can bear.

Fact: Your faith is a personal matter that only you can decide upon. It might help relieve your pain at times. However, there is no guarantee that spirituality and healing after a loss are linked. As for the second statement, sometimes the burden of loss can be greater than what you are equipped for. Accepting that you need help is vital for moving on.

Myth #22: Women grieve more than men.

Fact: The myth is not sex-specific. Women might grieve less or only as much as men. Sometimes, men grieve more. Gender is only a construct, most psychologists and social scientists would say. Grief has everything to do with a person and their nature. It doesn't matter whether you are a man or a woman—you deserve the chance to grieve and heal in either case.

Myth #23: Antidepressants and medication can help with grief.

Fact: Grief does not ordinarily require any medication. Numbing grief with medication, alcohol, or other drugs can delay the normal grieving process. It is only in cases where grief leads to depression or complicated grief that a medically trained professional might write certain drugs for you.

The above is not even a comprehensive list of myths that abound about grieving. You can find similar myths and the corresponding facts online. What is important to remember is that grieving is subjective and that no two people experience the same thing in exactly the same way.

In the last section of this chapter, we will consider one pervasive myth in more detail—a common misconception that many of us bear. We will look at how grieving, mourning, and depression are related but not the same things.

Grieving, Mourning, and Depression

Though grieving and mourning are related to loss and are often used interchangeably, they don't mean the same thing. Grieving is a more internal process of how you deal with the loss psychologically and emotionally. Mourning is usually an external marking of your grief. For instance, praying at the funeral could be mourning, while feeling sad and listless over the coming days is a part of your grieving process. Wearing black to show respect for the dead is part of your mourning while feeling angry or guilty could be part of your grieving.

Grieving is a more instinctive or emotional response to your loss than mourning is. In other words, mourning is how you choose to give your grieving a sense of direction. People choose to hold funerals, talk about their loved ones, institute memorials for them, or plant trees in their honor. These are all part of the mourning process. To put it simply, you have more control over how you want to mourn your loss than over how you want to grieve your loss. This isn't to say that you have absolutely no control over the grieving process. However, grief is more intuitive and reflexive than mourning.

Depression and grief are not to be confused. Depression is a psychological condition where a person is unable to exercise any control over their emotions. It is a clinical disorder that takes over a person's body and needs to be treated. There is no self-healing from depression. The following are some symptoms of depression that will help you understand it better:

- Sadness, anxiety, or emptiness that you carry with yourself most of the time

- Feeling a lack of pleasure in life and things you generally enjoyed

- Fatigue, low energy, and feeling bogged down

- Sleeping too much or too little

- Changes in appetite that lead to sudden weight gain or loss

- Constant inability to make decisions, remember things, or focus

- A lingering sense of hopelessness and gloom, no matter what you do

- Feeling unworthy, helpless, or guilty

- Feeling like harming yourself or suicidal

As you might have observed, some of these traits are similar to the complicated or long-term grief that we already discussed in the previous chapter. Depression requires a person to undergo either therapy, prescription medication, or a combination of both. It requires professional help and training to combat it. If you feel your grieving is leading to any or some of the symptoms above, then it is best to consult a medically trained professional to help you deal with it.

The following are some other reasons that may necessitate consulting a grief counselor or a therapist:

- You feel like you don't want to continue living.

- You wish you, too, had died with your loved one.

- You feel intensely responsible for the death of the person you lost.

- The numbness and shock won't wear off, and you can't seem to connect with people anymore.

- You don't feel like trusting people anymore.

- You feel dysfunctional and unable to do normal things.

Grief needs time. How much time it takes depends on the person who is grieving. Do not despair; the pain of your loss will remain as intensely strong as you feel it now. It is possible to work through it, and we will look at means of doing exactly this in the coming chapters.

Key Takeaways

- Traditionally, grief has five stages associated with it, though not everyone goes through it linearly. The five stages of grief serve to highlight how it is accompanied by various emotions at different points in time.

- Do not give in to any myth related to grieving. Let nobody judge you for how long or how you choose to grieve.

- Grieving is the internal reaction to loss, while mourning is the external way in which you choose to exhibit your grief. Depression is a clinical ailment that could or need not be related to loss. Depression requires medical assistance.

In Chapter 3, we will continue on our journey toward self-healing to look at practical tips on dealing with the complexity of emotions that loss gives rise to.

Coping With Grief and Emotional Turmoil

Give the sorrow words; the grief that does not speak knits up the o-er wrought heart and bids it break. –William Shakespeare

Despite being a trained doctor, Sangeeta Mahajan was unprepared for the severity with which her son's bipolar disorder progressed. When he committed suicide, she was left reeling from the aftermath of it. She describes the day as an ordinary one, though she does remember not wanting to go to work on that day. Her son was ill, and their family was back in India. All his friends had moved on to university, while he had stayed back home after completing two years owing to his mental health. She felt it was safe to leave him because he was on the right medicines, and his doctors had said that his progress was on the right track.

When Sangeetha got back home, all she had left of him was an apology note, which said that he was finding it hard to cope with it all. Her remorse and guilt at not having stayed by his side that day were crippling. All she wanted to do was hug him and tell him one last time how much she loved him. She kept wishing that she could turn back time and reverse the horrible thing that had happened.

She used her experience to become a mental health activist and runs a blog for suicide prevention and to help people deal with loss. She chose to deal with her devastating loss by sharing her experience with other parents and individuals who may be going through similar situations. She decided that her son must live on in her crusade against the destigmatizing of mental health issues. Today, her endeavor has helped her reach out to thousands of people who struggle with mental health and related problems (Mahajan, n.d.).

People have different ways in which they deal with grief. In this chapter, we will explore practical strategies that may help you move past your grief. Remember, not all the tips may work for you; you can use the techniques here to develop your own unique coping mechanism.

Expressing Grief and Other Emotions

There is a word commonly used in the context of a play or movie. "Catharsis" means the purification or cleansing of emotions via their expression. When you watch a movie or play, it helps you to feel and express some of the emotions that you might have been holding back. When you experience loss, you feel a surge of several powerful emotions, and sometimes you don't know what to do with them. Catharsis can be a helpful tool for letting them out so that our minds and bodies can be at ease.

Catharsis is linked to emotional healing because it enables a person to free up mental and physical energy by not withholding what they truly feel. It releases the negative energy associated with your loss. Since the times of Freud, catharsis has been linked to therapy and the purging of buried trauma in patients (Mukherjee, 2022).

In common parlance, what does catharsis mean, and more importantly, is it possible to achieve it in daily life? When we talk from the standpoint of undergoing grief, catharsis is an emotional release. As for the second question, the answer is a resounding "yes!" One can work towards releasing the pent-up suffering and turmoil healthily.

Communicating Loss to a Personal Circle

There is nothing as powerful as communicating your loss. If you can find a safe circle of friends or family who understand and do not judge you for it, it can be a very liberating experience.

The following are some things to keep in mind when you express your grief:

You should feel comfortable and ready. Do not let people guilt-trip you into speaking about your loss, nor allow unwanted people into your deepest feelings without your consent. When you are ready to speak about it, choose people like friends and family members who can support you through the process. People who invalidate or trivialize your experiences will only add to your burden of grief. Even with people, you feel safe around, it is always good to constantly check in with yourself about how much and how soon you want to reveal the full extent of your problems. This is not to discourage you from talking openly but merely to remind you to talk at your own pace.

Prepare yourself mentally. Grief and its mechanizations cannot be forced or hurried. Thus, be honest with yourself about whether you are ready to open up. Ask yourself questions such as:

- Am I ready to talk about my grief?

- Will I be able to answer the questions my listeners may want to ask?

- Do I have the emotional strength to go through with it?

- Do I believe myself to have the patience or mental stability to withstand the process?

If you are unsure about any one of the questions above, you can choose to postpone your discussion. You are the best judge of whether you are ready for the leap.

Write your feelings down. We will come to grief journals in the next chapter. Even if you aren't the journaling type, you can use a pen and paper to jot down the major points of your experience that you would like to express to a trusted person. This will aid in staying focused on what you want to express without rambling. After having avoided people for a while, you may struggle with saying the right things. This step will help you clarify your thoughts and feelings and find the words to say exactly what you want to say. Some people also choose to write letters or emails to friends and family whom they would rather not face yet. This is also an option that you can explore. Writing can be a cathartic release too.

There is no need to feel guilty about your emotions or to downplay them. You are talking about your grief to people whom you trust. You should own your emotions. Be willing to accept all your emotions. You are not obligated to suppress your feelings to make them comfortable. If they are true friends, they will support you in your courage to be vulnerable. You need to feel relaxed enough to open up to them, and when you do, there is no need to hide your true self. Don't let others tell you things like to "chin up" or not to "overreact."

Be clear about your needs. When somebody asks you questions that you would rather not answer or makes a comment that upsets you, explain honestly to them why certain things are still hard for you to navigate. You have the right to set your boundaries as the grieving person and to let them know that, though you appreciate their good intentions, you will not tolerate interference. You can gently explain when their efforts are in keeping with your way of grieving and when they are not.

Personal support from friends and family members can be a huge blessing to someone grieving. However, there may be times when you crave the anonymity of the help you receive or when friends and family members are at a loss for how to support you. This is where professional help comes in. In the next section, we look at why you should not be too hasty in rejecting therapy and when you should seek it.

Seeking Professional Help: When and Why?

One of the best yardsticks to measure whether you need "outside" professional or medical help is when you feel dysfunctional over a long period of time. But how do you identify how long that is or what being dysfunctional means? Moreover, what can a stranger do for me that I myself, or friends and family, haven't been able to do? This section will help you answer some questions you may have in this regard.

The following is a roadmap of expectations for what grief looks like, and though it is never the same for any two people, you might recognize some patterns in it.

Time After Loss	Experience
1 Month	You experience numbness and shock. You live on autopilot, and though you can get things done, you hardly know how you're managing.
2–3 Months	People have returned to their normal routines, and you suddenly realize your loss. You might feel stuck in your grief, unable to focus or do things that you would normally do. You may feel emotional, upset, and unable to sleep or eat.
4–6 Months	There may be a few better days now, but the intensity of your grief outbursts takes you by surprise. Around the 6-month mark, you may relapse into grief again because of a first birthday, holiday, or anniversary on which your loved one isn't around.
7–12 Months	Bad days will come and go, but you feel better overall as more moments of hope and joy come in. There is the dread of the first anniversary of your loss looming ahead. But sometimes, the day isn't as bad as you expected it to be.
Second Year	The second year after the anniversary could be better or worse than the first. People are surprised at the intense grief that still comes over them at times.

Sometimes, you observe that the loss you experienced is falling further behind you in time, but your coping strategies are repeatedly failing, or you are simply unable to cope with daily things you managed earlier without giving them a second thought. This is one of the first yellow flags to consider when deciding whether you need therapy or grief counseling.

The other reasons you might want to consider therapy are when you have no loved ones to support you or if they are inaccessible to you. Perhaps you find yourself struggling with new roles and responsibilities owing to your loss. Long-term problems with sleeping, such as oversleeping, waking up frequently, the inability to fall asleep, etc., can lead to severe energy slumps during the day. This will prevent you from leading a full life. Similarly, if you find yourself engaging in destructive or self-destructive thoughts, it is a red flag and an indication that you need professional help.

To answer the question as to why grief therapy works when other self-help methods fail, we will look at some of the coping methods that therapy applies.

Grief counseling focuses on acceptance of the loss. The time we spend in numbed disbelief and shock can be more effectively channeled into an awareness of our loss and in trying to foresee how it might affect us. This will greatly help in feeling a better sense of preparedness for facing the challenges that lie ahead.

Secondly, grief counseling paves the way to work through the grief of loss. The counselor, who knows your past, interests, and hobbies thoroughly, will help you discover the most effective ways in which you can express your grief and find an outlet for it. A therapist will know of a variety of methods you can explore for this purpose. You don't have to start your search for the right method on your own or from scratch.

One of the best parts of therapy is its focus on adjusting to life in the face of your loss. Whether it is the loss of a loved one, a job, or a home, you will learn specific strategies to move on in life without this person, place, or thing in your life. This can help you heal faster, experiment, and partake in new pleasures in life.

Grief counseling is also about maintaining a connection with the loved one you have lost while still trying to rebuild your life. With your help, your counselor will help you frame methods to remember your loved one constructively, which will help you in your journey to self-discovery.

Some of the more specific ways in which counselors can tap into your grief are:

- Allowing you to talk about the loved one and how their loss has affected you via guided sessions.

- Encouraging you to express your emotions and feelings.

- Guiding you in building coping strategies for tough days such as anniversaries or birthdays.

- Outlining the grieving process and teaching you what to expect from it.

- Helping you to identify unhealthy behaviors and seek remedies for them.

- Assisting you in finding new relationships and a new self-identity.

These are some of the several ways in which counseling or medical support can complement or be more helpful than the support of friends and family.

In the next section, we will delve into what you can do by way of self-care practices to help ease the pain of grief.

Self-Care Practices

We talk about self-care today in virtually every situation. It helps combat stress, anxiety, and the onset of depression. Thus, it is equally important where the handling of grief is concerned. Since we spoke about grief in terms of physical, emotional, behavioral, and mental symptoms, we will look at self-care practices that can alleviate each of these.

Physical Self-Care

I don't have to tell you that your body requires fuel, rest, and plenty of exercise for it to remain active, healthy, and happy. This is more true when it undergoes stressors, such as a big and unexpected loss. The three keys to keeping your body running are eating, sleeping, and exercising well.

Feed yourself healthy, nutritious, and comforting foods during grief. It is easy to forget meals during such periods. However, get the help of a friend to remind you to eat well. You don't have to spend time on elaborate cooking if you don't feel like it. Instead, ensure that you eat plenty of vegetables, fruits, and protein-rich items, and cut back on unhealthy snacking. Though you may be tempted to eat sugary and fried items, refrain from doing so. Keep to a strict schedule where meals are concerned. Unhealthy eating patterns add to the stress that your body is undergoing. Drink plenty of water or other fluids. Keeping hydrated will help you remain calmer in the face of your grief. Dehydration can add to the physical and mental strain you feel.

Sleep is one of the harder things that people struggle with. Though no tactic is foolproof at granting you good sleep during this period, you can try sticking to a schedule, cutting out light and sound, and using white noise to fall asleep. Get rid of gadgets in your room so that you aren't tempted to check your phone or switch on the TV when you wake up. The glare of these devices disrupts your sleep cycle even during normal times.

Listen to your body and its needs. There are days when it will ask you to be more active or to engage in things around you. There may be other days when it seems to be asking you to rest or sleep. Do whatever it takes to keep your body happy. A fit body is where a healthy mind can reside too.

Exercising and getting some sunshine is a great way of reconnecting with your body and also getting out of your head. I understand it may not be something that comes naturally after losing something you held dear. However, if you push yourself a little, you may perhaps even find happiness in it eventually. Our bodies were designed to move and do things. When it is deprived of this activity, it can feel even more depressing.

Progressive muscle relaxation and body scanning are effective ways to help yourself come to terms with the physical aches and discomforts of grief. Here, you focus on each muscle group from your head to your toes, or vice versa, and spend time trying to relax it. People claim a reduction in physical pain after using this therapeutic method.

Emotional Self-Care

Taking care of your emotional needs is significantly more important when you are grieving. We discussed catharsis and how it can help with emotional healing. Apart from talking to loved ones or seeking professional help, you can think of some of the methods below to give you emotional sustenance.

Music is a great way of releasing tension. It helps relax both the body and the mind. Some people swear by playing music according to their moods to help with catharsis. For instance, a sad song to help with pain, or a peppy number when you are happy, etc. Select music that is soothing for you, and try to keep aside all distractions, especially intrusive thoughts, when you are listening to it.

Art therapy, such as crafts or sculpting, can help release tension. It is also one of the most productive ways to channel your grief. People find it a huge relief to be able to paint, sculpt, or write about their loved ones. We will be covering this aspect in more detail in the next chapter.

The punching bag method is normally an effective way to combat the more powerful emotions associated with anger, such as grief. If you can imagine the punching bag as the people you consider responsible for your loss, the act of physically venting your anger will help you calm down.

Psychodrama provides an outlet for your emotions as you reenact the painful scenes from your loss and revisit your pain. You may need the help of a professional or someone else to do this. Eventually, this method can help you let go of suffering, trauma, and the residual feelings of grief.

Volunteering for social causes can help you focus on a larger cause as you deal with your pain and grief. Many choose to remember their loved ones through the service and sacrifices they make by serving others. We will look at specific ways to honor yourself and your loss in Chapter 5.

Spiritual Self-Care

This is a very personal side of how you choose to deal with grief. Some people turn to religion and find solace there. Others turn away from spirituality and instead decide to focus on more concrete things. Either way, you get to decide your beliefs and where your faith lies.

Spirituality is often confused with being religious. Yet, that is not the only way one can be spiritual. It can encompass a variety of philosophical questions, such as whether you consider yourself a good person, what you consider to be your purpose in life, how you can live your best life, and so on. The answers you frame for these questions define your spirituality.

Spirituality can also be trying to find a connection between your actions and how they can shape something bigger than yourself. It has less to do with your emotions and more to do with your idea of your soul and where it lies.

Mental Self-Care

This last part of self-care deals with keeping your mind and cognitive processes sharp. While undergoing grief and its associated emotions, many people slip into a mental fog of not being able to focus on what is happening around them. Thinking, making rational decisions, and problem-solving take a hit in these circumstances. The following are some ways to maintain your mental health, especially after a loss.

Reading books and magazines on topics you enjoy can keep your mental faculties sharp. If you want to read about coping with loss, that would be great. However, you don't have to force yourself into the genre. You can engage in light reading if you don't want to get into heavy or serious subjects at the moment.

Watching movies or other entertainment programs can be a great way to keep your mind active. Select subjects or genres that you prefer, and ensure you keep all extraneous thoughts away as you focus on the movie. Watching humorous movies or series can also boost your overall mood. Some people claim that tragic content allows for emotional catharsis. However, the idea is for you to feel at ease. Don't watch anything that may further disturb your tranquility.

Puzzles and words, video, and board games can keep your mind engaged and briefly off your sorrow. These also exercise specific parts of your brain and can help improve your focus, even through your sadness. If you find playing on your own tough, get a friend to play with you so that you stay involved in it.

Ultimately, coping with a painful loss is a voyage wherein you have to steer yourself based on what seems to work best for you.

Key Takeaways

- One of the fastest ways to heal yourself is to talk about your grief to trusted friends and family members when you are ready, in the manner you choose.

- Professional help should be sought when it is necessary. There is no substitute for this when it is needed. Keep checking your symptoms and the progress of your healing to see whether you need counseling.

- Self-care is the best policy when you are grieving. Self-care includes mental, emotional, physical, and spiritual practices that will enable you to find peace in what might otherwise seem like an extremely chaotic and stressful time.

In the next chapter, we will examine concrete tools and techniques that will help you cope with grief.

Chapter 4:

Tools and Techniques for Healing

The most beautiful people we have known are those who have known defeat, known suffering, known struggle, known loss, and have found their way out of the depths. These persons have an appreciation, a sensitivity, and an understanding of life that fills them with compassion, gentleness, and a deep loving concern. Beautiful people do not just happen. –Elizabeth Kubler Ross

Nilsa Rivera Castro reveals how mixed-media art and journaling helped her find balance and healing by combining various forms of art. She speaks of how she dealt with her depression by writing more. It opened up a "sealed compartment of her soul." When she wanted to express her emotions in an even more tangible or physical form, she started dabbling in art therapy. She brushed, splashed, and created works that transformed and cleansed her deep, dark feelings into joy and love.

She used paper, gels, paints, pictures from magazines, and other raw materials to create pages of art. During the process, she also discovered that initially, her paintings were mostly black and red, which represented her innate fear, violence, anger, and aggression. However, the more she painted, the more she could experiment with a more varied palette. Today, she has found mental, physical, and emotional equilibrium by using colors and words. She tells us that it wasn't a therapist who advised her to engage in art therapy but rather her listening to the needs of her body, mind, and soul that enabled her to achieve peace (Castro, 2018).

Psychology has established the therapeutic benefits of art and journaling. At the center of this therapy lies the idea that it is possible to transmute your pain, grief, and every other negative emotion into something new. This can be the beginning of healing and imparting purpose to your life.

In this chapter, we will focus on some of the techniques that we only hinted at earlier—their benefits, drawbacks, and how they contribute to your healing.

Journaling

Keeping a grief journal is a great way to get started on providing an outlet for your grief. It doesn't require you to purchase too many things, either. All you need is a diary and a few pens to set the activity in motion. More importantly, you will need to dedicate time during the day to sit down and vent to your thoughts, emotions, and feelings. This could be the hardest part of the process because it requires some discipline that you may have to initially force upon yourself until the routine becomes a part of your existence. Let us try to understand better why a grief journal will help you.

Unlike speaking, which is more instantaneous and spontaneous, writing allows you to put your thoughts in order, reflect upon them, and decide how exactly you would like to present them. Automatically, then, writing provides you with the scope to clarify, organize, and work through your thoughts and feelings. As you write, you may also recognize certain patterns within your thought processes. Many say that writing something down helps them get it out of their systems. If you find yourself thinking in circles or are unable to extricate yourself from rut thinking, writing could be your solution.

One of our biggest fears related to the loss of a dear person is whether we will forget them. When your memories and feelings are still flush with grief, writing them down will help you capture the essence of your loved one, as it will help remind you later how exactly the grief felt at the time. Writing is one of the best memorials you can provide for your loved one and for the grief you feel. It will help keep their memory alive and make you feel closer to them. This can be a comforting feeling, indeed.

Ordinarily, journaling has a lot to do with keeping track of your progress. The same is true where grief is concerned. As you turn the pages of your journal, you will realize how far you have come in managing and channeling your grief more productively or creatively. It will also fill you with a sense of gratitude and confidence that, though your loss is heavy, you are able to carry it bravely and see it through to the end.

Every kind of journaling reduces the stress of having to go through convoluted, unclear thinking and feelings. Journaling will help you look at things from a new perspective and will give your emotions and ideas new permutations and combinations, which will help you troubleshoot and calm yourself better.

So, what can you do to start keeping a grief journal?

Choose a journal that will help you most to express yourself. Some people use diaries or notebooks, while others use notes on their phones or the word processor on their laptops. There is no right or wrong way of maintaining a journal. Some benefit more from the use of a pen on paper because they claim the physical act of writing can give them a cathartic release that isn't so obvious with typing. When you intend to pen longer pieces, the traditional way of writing could be more effective because there is no added strain of staring into the glare of the screen for that long.

Take baby steps at a time. This is not a contest where you have to complete a minimum of so many words. Start small by writing a sentence or two every day. Even writing for a few minutes a day can make a difference in the way you process your grief. When you engage with shorter pieces, try to select your words or sentences intentionally to depict what you are feeling most at the moment.

Don't limit your writing to subjects you think should be directly related to your grief. You can write about what you did during the day, memories, or lists of people and situations that make you angry. This is a space where you can speak your mind honestly.

Reread your writing. This is not so much for the sake of editing as to engage with your healing journey. When you go back to your writing from a few days or weeks ago, it will help you realize how you are making progress in your struggle with grief.

Choose the audience for whom you are writing. Expressing your grief to a certain individual will have you refine and prune your writing for their sake. You can also try writing the same incident for different readers, anticipating the kinds of questions that they might ask you. This will help you see things from a fresh angle.

Some prompts that you can perhaps use to start are:

1. In my overwhelming grief, I am grateful for...

2. If this letter could find my loved one, I would tell them...

3. Today, the one thing I really miss is...

4. I will be more compassionate to myself in the following ways...

5. I know I am feeling better now because...

Your journal is a reflection of who you are. Thus, you can write about whatever comes to your mind. We will now explore mindfulness and meditation for alleviating grief.

Mindfulness and Meditation

Simply explained, mindfulness is being aware of every sensation, thought, feeling, and emotion in you at a given moment. For instance, you can choose to eat your food with half your mind on it as you mindlessly scroll through your social media account. You can also choose to set aside your phone and devote all your senses to the texture, taste, smell, and color of the food you are eating. You might even hear the sound of it as you chew on it. The latter is when you are eating mindfully. Mindfulness can be applied in all aspects of life, including grieving. Building an awareness of your body, mind, and feelings through your healing process will help you surmount grief and find new meaning in life after your loss. Let us first list how mindfulness can aid your journey to wellness.

It helps in accepting your feelings. One of the first steps to living mindfully is to acknowledge our feelings honestly and openly. This helps, especially with the stages of shock, anger, and depression when you are in denial of or grappling with your emotions. Mindfulness will help us come to terms with what we are feeling. If I were to frame this in a sentence, it could look like I feel heavy/sad/angry/anxious/restless today. It is normal to feel this way because I have lost something or someone important to me."

Mindfulness can be practiced to become a part of everything that you do daily in your life. For instance, if you choose to journal or take part in a physical activity, you should be wholly engaged in it. You will tell yourself that all other considerations and thoughts can come after you have given your whole mind to the task at hand. For instance, you might say, "I love how my handwriting looks on this paper. I will now devote this time to writing to the best of my abilities right now."

Reaching out to people—personal or professional acquaintances—can be done mindfully. For example, when you need to talk about your grief, you may either select somebody you are close to or a more impersonal person, like a counselor who will listen to you without judgment. At different points in your healing path, you will face the need to be both alone with your grief and to reach out to people. You get to choose which of these you want at a particular moment.

You can choose to take care of yourself mindfully. We already discussed physical, emotional, mental, and spiritual ways to take care of yourself. Whatever routine you decide on, you have to be fully present in it. Your five senses and your mind have to be part of your healing process. Mindful self-care will hasten your joy in life.

Mindfully celebrating or commemorating the life of the person you have lost can also be a wonderful way of finding purpose and meaning in life again. This will help you trace how you have grown by being beside them and provide a tribute to the unique relationship you shared with them. We will be covering this last form of mindfulness in more detail in the next chapter.

Since we spent some time on mindfulness, we will now look at a term that is often used synonymously with it—meditation. Meditation is related to mindfulness but is not the same as it. Mindfulness is a practice, while meditation is a mental exercise rooted in mindfulness. Meditation is the art of being able to focus on one thing alone. This may sound easy, but those who have tried it will tell you how challenging it can be. Our minds are often compared to monkeys frolicking on the branches of trees. It is an extremely hard task to pin down your mind or hold it still. This is what meditation aims at. More experienced practitioners of meditation learn the art of keeping their minds completely blank for a period of time. In other words, they can suspend their thoughts and feelings completely for this duration.

Meditation helps the mind relax. It reduces stress, anxiety, and other negative thoughts and feelings around our loss. Since meditation helps decrease stress, it also increases the immunity of your body in the long run. When we meditate, we sit with our feelings and hold them there until their presence becomes a part of us. This helps with accepting our emotions, even if they are negative. Meditation improves our ability to focus and make good decisions. This may help with clearing the mental fog that grief brings in its wake. Research has tentatively established the links between meditation and better sleep, both in quality and quantity (Rusch et al., 2019). If you want to find rest in your grief, meditation is an excellent practice. It can also provide relief from sensations such as aches, pains, and muscle cramps, improving the overall quality of your physical health.

If you plan to use meditation, keep in mind the following points:

- Select a comfortable space devoid of noise and clutter that is airy and bright.

- There is no particular pose that you need to assume for meditation. It would be most comfortable to sit down. However, if you want to experiment by standing or lying down, you can do that as well. The rule of thumb is that you should be comfortable and in no danger of dozing off.

- You can use music or a recorded mantra if that helps you focus better.

- When you start, you can look at an object in front of you before closing your eyes and holding it in your mind.

- Throughout your meditation, ensure that you inhale slowly through your nose and exhale deeply and slowly through your mouth. Let your breathing continue at a normal and relaxed pace. Experts suggest the use of belly or diaphragmatic breathing, wherein you expand and contract your abdomen each time you inhale and exhale respectively.

- As you become better at concentrating on an object, try to erase even that image and not think of anything. When you find your mind jumping from limb to limb, ground yourself by bringing your attention back to your breathing.

- If you find holding your mind blank difficult, try the body scanning technique we already mentioned in the last chapter. You can focus on each muscle group starting at either end of your body. Simply observe how different parts of your body feel or sense things around it. Keep breathing until you feel the tightness easing in areas where you may feel some discomfort.

- You can meditate for any duration of your choice in a day. With constant practice, you will find it easier and more enjoyable.

In the last major part of this chapter, we look at various ways in which your grief can be converted into creative outlets.

Creative Expression

Humanity has used creativity to surmount challenges since time immemorial. One of the first things that humans started doing when they discovered communication and writing was to draw rudimentary pictures on the walls of their dwellings. We have come a long way from then, and our art forms have only become more diverse, complex, and beautiful.

Artistic expression is a great way of providing cathartic release to a person suffering from any kind of pain. Its power, depth, and ability to cure are often undermined. However, we shall consider some types of creative channels and how they could help you.

- Music therapy can help a person immensely. This includes either listening to or creating music. Learning an instrument or going to vocal classes may help you create a safe outlet for your emotions.

- Dancing is both a physical exercise as well as a creative medium of self-expression. Apart from letting steam off, dancing will help you focus better on your body's movements in sync with the music.

- Drama can also be a powerful tool. With the combination of dialogue delivery and emoting on stage, actors can bring characters to life on paper. In one of the earlier chapters, we talked about psychodrama, which is an extension of role-playing and acting.

- Memorial tattoos can help etch a lost person into the skin of their survivor. This can be a way to remember the person and also your journey in surviving this loss.

- Narrating or storytelling helps people express their grief by telling their own or others' stories. This can help improve communication and emotional regulation.

- Painting, doodling, drawing, or making photo essays or collages is a great way of depicting the emotions and complexity of your thoughts in the face of the grief you hold inside. Creating such artwork will help you release the tension your body holds.

- Sculpting, metalworking, woodworking, and carpentry are other ways in which people choose to memorialize their pain or the loved ones lost. The finished products of your efforts will remain a monument to your loss and the love you have for them.

As for the scientific efficacy of whether art does heal, studies have shown it to help reduce trauma, depression, and the psychological effects of cancer and to improve self-esteem (Cherry, 2023).

Some things to remember if you plan to explore art therapy are:

- You don't have to be an artist or have formal training in art to express your thoughts and emotions through it.

- People who consider themselves poor artists sometimes find it harder to overcome their resistance to art therapy. It isn't for everyone and won't work unless you believe strongly in its curative powers.

- Though you can do it at home, with the help of online tutorials to get some ideas, you can approach qualified art therapists who are doubly qualified in psychology and art. Most of these therapists will also have areas of expertise such as trauma, grief, substance abuse, etc. You can choose someone you think will help with your particular problem.

- If your art therapist is certified, your insurance or other medical waivers may cover them. This is not guaranteed, of course, but you can check it out as an option.

- During the first couple of classes, your therapist will try to get to know you better. They will ask you questions about your background and your specific type of grief. Based on these, they will ask you to explore certain types of art: painting, writing, etc.

- You will need to talk about your art. A large part of art therapy is explaining your work and its significance with respect to your life. You may have to think of how doing it made you feel, whether it stirred any memories, and what you think of your work now that you have completed it.

On the whole, writing and art become potent tools for catharsis and self-expression when you are mindfully engaged in the process. The key is to learn that the more rooted you are in your present and doing productive work in which you find beauty and fulfillment, the easier it will be to navigate your grief.

Key Takeaways

We reviewed some of the most common ways in which people successfully maneuver through their loss and grief cycles.

- Journaling your thoughts and emotions can build clarity and lay the foundation for communicating your grief.

- Mindfulness will enable you to be present in the here and now of things. Meditation is one particular exercise that will strengthen your ability to be mindful.

- Art therapy is an avenue to explore the intricacies of your grief while producing meaningful and creative outcomes.

In the next chapter, we will look at ways in which you can honor yourself, your loss, and your grief.

Chapter 5:

Some Tips to Honor Yourself and Your Loss

Death ends a life, not a relationship. –Mitch Albom

Michelle talks of a very traumatic loss that she encountered in her freshman year of high school when her brother Tom, who was 27 years old, committed suicide. He had been battling schizophrenia. To add to her grief, which she did not feel immediately, she felt "watched" by her small community, which had never experienced a loss of this kind. She imagined that people were talking about her family and was unprepared for the anger, guilt, and shame she felt. She felt like crawling into a hole and never coming out again, despite the fact that she wanted to have friends who loved her and support her. This wasn't the end of it. Two years later, in her senior year of college, her dad died of a rare lung cancer.

She put on a brave face through the normal things a soon-to-be college student should enjoy, like prom and parties, though on the inside, she felt as if she were crumbling. Her trauma led her to often imagine seeing her dad's face in a crowd, only to be disappointed later when she discovered that it wasn't him. She tells us how for a long time, she used secluded places on her campus and her shower to cry out her grief. She did not want to let others in on her suffering.

She also gets real when talking about the symptoms of grief: exhaustion, lethargy, and a lack of focus. While she had been a student who got straight A's in high school, she couldn't keep up with her college work. Finally, it was a college support group for other grievers like her where she finally found that she could fit in. Michelle completed her Masters in Mental Health Counseling and holds a

Certificate in Thanatology, the study of death and dying (Servaty-Seib & Lynn, 2015). Working as a bereavement counselor, she feels that this is the work destined for her. She feels that though her losses changed her life, they gave her a sense of purpose and direction too.

In this chapter, we look at some ways in which you can give time to grief and still be yourself through the whole process. Grieving does not necessarily mean that your life has come to a standstill. You can continue to live while acknowledging and accepting the pain you feel.

Some Tips for You

Let me start with the disclaimer that the following is not a complete list of tips on how you can manage your grief. These are only intended to work as pointers toward your unique path toward self-healing. Most importantly, keep in mind that you can modify, change, or remove routines that you feel are not working for you. Ultimately, this is your journey, and you get to decide how to conduct yourself.

Memorialize Your Loved One

There are many ways to memorialize your loved one. And we will explore a few ones that seem to give many a respite from their grief.

Keep a little of them alive in the things they leave behind. In olden times, people would preserve a lock of hair from a loved one who passed on. You don't have to do exactly that. You can hold on to the clothes they possess or refashion them into something you can use. We all keep photos of them framed in our bedroom or on the mantelpiece. It can be an article of daily wear as well. For instance, it could be their reading glasses, or some ornament they wore, etc. Some have memorial rings or lockets that hold a part of the remains of their loved ones. You can also make a memory book about them with pictures of items that they loved.

There are other ways of keeping the memory of a loved one alive, such as by donating to a cause that is close to their heart or by establishing a charity in their name.

Some people want to pay a living tribute to their loved ones by planting a tree or a garden in honor of the one they lost.

You can also start a new tradition to mark the loss of a loved one. For instance, the whole family can decide to gather at home to remember the person each year on their anniversary or reach out to each other that day.

Think of all the things that interested the person you lost, using which you can conduct events such as choirs, book exhibitions, etc. in their memory.

Change one thing about their life that they would have wanted from you. For instance, there are children who decide to turn a new leaf and become better people after the loss of their parents. A friend I knew was smoking after the day his mother passed away because she had been telling him to do it for years.

Weave Your Story

Telling your story orally or in a written format can be a great way of giving shape to your grief. Your words and experience could help others in their grieving journey as well. Grief journals, which we already discussed, can help you collect your thoughts whenever you are ready to tell your story to the world. The story of your loved one or your loss is also the story of your history together. It can include the good, bad, and ugly. You don't have to sugarcoat anything, fearing that you are "dishonoring" their memory. Telling the truth is a cathartic experience that you deserve. Think of questions that you will need to address yourself, such as:

- How should your life look now after your loss?

- What would you like to pursue hereafter?

- What are the thoughts worrying you most right now?

- Was your loss expected or unexpected?

- Who is your primary support group?

If you can answer the above questions, you will be able to depict your loss eloquently in words. Remember, you never know when your story could become helpful for another person like you. The mistake we often make is telling ourselves that nobody will be interested in our story or that we can't bring ourselves to talk about our loss. Many times, just the process of sorting out the jumble of our thoughts and feelings will motivate us to share the story.

Establish a Routine

No matter how intense and unbearable your feelings may seem at this moment, it is essential to put in place a routine as early as possible. I know that it may not seem like the time to think of such a thing, but this is one of the basic survival tactics that will hold you in good stead. There must be fixed times for meals, walking the dog, resting, and getting some form of physical exercise. A schedule will help you not think too much about what to do next. It will simplify your life so that you can set aside time to focus on things that matter to you.

Another thing that may help you is to visually imagine your "worry boxes." This is a way of compartmentalizing your grief and putting a lid on a certain worry that may be hindering you from living a full life right now. When you create these worry boxes, you can choose not to get anxious over all your problems at once. You can, instead, tackle one thing at a time. It is just a way to organize your feelings of distress better. It will also give you a better sense of control over everything.

Jotting down a to-do list of things to be covered is also an excellent way of getting a grip on the mundane things that a loss can entail. Remember, this does not in any way mean that you are not grieving. It simply means that you are trying your best to put your life back together—a task that is as brave as it is necessary.

Be Kind to Yourself

Though I did say that you should establish a routine and be kind to yourself when you aren't always able to stick to it, keeping your commitments is a good way of negotiating some time away from your grief. However, don't overbook yourself with so many things to do that you have no time for yourself. This will make it impossible to find the time and space necessary to heal.

Resting more than usual is not a sign of weakness. This is your system telling you that you need to slow down and recover your mind and body. There is no shame in this. As we already mentioned, self-care routines will greatly help you to root yourself through the incredibly tough days.

Set Aside Time to Grieve

Keep aside time daily to think about the person or thing you lost. Do what it takes to "let out" the pain that is holding you hostage. We often think that talking about pain is only for people who have had great relationships with the person, job, or place they lost. However, the pain of loss can affect you even when you have a troubled relationship with your lost past. For instance, you finally had the courage to resign from a job that you knew was not serving you. You think that once you stop going to work, you will automatically feel better. However, the fact is that you might miss the mundane routine of the job you held. The uncertainty of the future, by comparison, may be scaring you. It is okay to feel your loss as you work toward a new and changed future.

Some things that you can do to clear your mind of the pain are:

- Sit quietly and bring to your mind the person or thing you lost.

- Play music or any other audio that helps you focus on your mental picture better.

- Imagine your loss is sitting right next to you and holding an imaginary conversation with them.

- Cry. It is the most natural way in which we grieve. Don't hold back on your crying.

- Write a journal or a letter about your loss.

Confront Barriers to Grief

You might be experiencing one or more barriers that are preventing you from expressing your grief. These could look different for different people. There is a misconception that focusing more on the barriers may help "resolve" them. It isn't often as simple as that. Some common barriers could include:

- **Anxiety**: Overthinking what you could have done differently to have avoided this loss or frequently asking, "Why me?" can be a barrier to your healing process. Books and stories often tell us that life is fair and that good people have good outcomes. Unfortunately, this isn't the case in real life. Life isn't always fair, and no matter how many times you think it ought to be a certain way, some things just don't have an explanation.

- **A lack of closure**: You may have unanswered questions over which your brain will think in circles. If you weren't at hand when a loved one dies, you often keep thinking back to their final moments, what they must have felt, and whether they felt any pain, etc. Even if you run over the known facts a million times, these are questions that will remain open forever.

- **Guilt, anger, and regret**: We did deal with these emotions as natural in the face of a loss. Yet, indulging them for longer than necessary will not help you get past the pain. It might be helpful to list down why you feel guilty, angry, or regretful and then use the facts of the situation to determine conclusively whether any other action on your part could have changed the outcome. In most cases, you will realize that what happened was out of your hands.

- **Avoidance of people or places**: This can be an early coping mechanism where grief is involved. You avoid people or places that you associate with your loss. You may avoid going to places that your loved one used to enjoy. Not being ready to face it is fine; however, complete avoidance for a long time will only make the healing process slower and more difficult.

- **Difficult decisions to be made**: Following a loss of any kind, there are many decisions that will require your attention. Holding a funeral, documents to be handled, finances to be settled, where you can stay, etc. There are some decisions that can't wait. Those are the ones you will have to make a call on with the aid of friends and family members. It's best not to make any major decisions in the first year of your loss. For instance, don't hurry to sell off your house after the death of a loved one.

One of the hardest but most necessary processes toward healing from loss is connecting with others.

Connect With People Who Understand

Memorial services are as much for the one who dies as the ones living. It gives everybody who cares about the dead an opportunity to come together and offer each other consolation during this painful time.

You can seek out others who have experienced a loss similar to yours. Hearing their stories will reveal similarities and differences between their and your coping processes. It might also give you ideas about trying out a new method of venting your grief. You will find people who uplift you in your low moments. Being of help to them could give your life a new purpose or meaning too.

You can also try to forge relationships with people who have moved past the worst of their suffering and can mentor you through yours. They might organize engagements and activities that will keep you occupied. Just having them for help and support might be the release you need too.

As we already mentioned, when life becomes too much, there is the option of getting professional help from psychotherapy or grief counseling as well. You can ask others who have been through therapy, members of the religious community you may be a part of, or friends and family members for recommendations on certified grief counselors. This will help you decide on a course of action as soon as possible.

Engage in Community Service

What better way to channel your grief than to use it to serve others? If you can find a charitable cause or be part of an NGO to serve others, it can be the most meaningful tribute you are paying to your loss. People talk about how raising awareness about the illness that killed their loved one, baking for the hungry and poor, or accumulating money and goods that may serve the needy helped them to feel at peace with themselves.

Apart from the service you are rendering to the community, this is also a great way to meet other people and find out what drove them to participate in the mission. Working with others toward a common goal will make it easier to reach out to people and make new friends. It will help you expand your social network and might allow you to learn new skills in the process. Involving your family in the same work will give you all the time to bond as well as to channel your grief as one.

Social work relieves stress and the baggage of negative emotions we carry around. It can thus promote your psychological well-being and actively combat depression. If you are an animal lover, working with pets or stray animals can bring a sense of love and joy into your life. There is research that proves that helping others gives the mind pleasure via the release of hormones that make you happy (Robinson & Segal, 2019).

Deal With the "Firsts" of Your Loss

The first anniversary of your loss, the birthday of a loved one who is no more, receiving a letter addressed to the one you lost, or meeting somebody who looks like the deceased are all situations in which you will find a resurgence of your grief. There will be other occasions, such as a graduation party, a wedding, or the birth of a child the loved one misses. Being prepared for these "firsts" on which your loved one can no longer be present is an important part of the mourning and healing journey.

There are four steps to tackling these firsts that may otherwise take you by surprise (Morris, 2017):

1. **Anticipate**: What are the events coming ahead? Where will you be present when they happen? Who are the people who will be around you at the time?

2. **Plan**: What do you want to do? Are there things you may have to arrange ahead of time?

3. **Set realistic expectations**: Are your expectations realistic, especially for Step 2? Have you overcommitted?

4. **Reminisce**: What memories do you want to share? With whom do you want to share them?

Next, we look at how spirituality can be a part of the question.

Embrace Religion or Spirituality—Does It Really Help?

There are people for whom an intense loss can awaken spiritual or religious feelings that existed prior to the incident. There are yet others who were already religious or spiritual and who turned it away, at least for a while, when they experienced the throes of loss. Neither way is correct or wrong. There are merely paths that work for you and do not. You are the best judge of how you can deal with your feelings and thoughts in the best manner.

The feeling that God has a path designed for you can be immensely consoling in the face of grief. Your belief in a higher spirit, even if you don't follow the tenets of any given school of religion, can firmly root you in a higher calling for yourself and allow you to tackle your emotions better after a loss. It could lend profundity to your experience, helping you heal faster. Many say that religion and rituals help them find a new meaning in their lives.

On the other hand, there is nothing wrong with believing that life is arbitrary and that random misfortunes can visit random people without any meaning. However, you should also be careful that you don't fall into a pit of despair, overthinking the futility of life. Even if a life you thought had promise was cut short in its prime, you can make yours count in the time you are given on this planet. In fact, the loss should help you see more clearly how you want to create meaning for yourself in your life.

Build New Roads

It can be hard to let go of the life you had fallen into before your loss. It was comfortable, secure, and known. The life ahead is unknown, and until you create a routine, it can seem scary. People often talk of the "two steps ahead, one step behind" method of coping with the new life. There will be days on which, no matter how hard you try to step forward, your grief will pull you back. However slow as the progress may be, by taking two steps, even if you fall one step behind, you will still get ahead of your initial position eventually.

There is no point in aiming to forget what you lost. That is not how the human psyche was crafted to be. Instead, you have to try to forge new memories and new schedules that will in time, help you live with the old memories. As you move ahead, you will find the connection between your old and new lives and stop treating them as two distinct and separate segments. You will also realize how the old life has prepared you for certain things now, and you will find yourself building upon them. Metaphorically speaking, it is like the construction of a new floor on an existing building rather than the demolition of an old structure to give way to a new one.

Have Fun

If you feel that having fun is an injustice to the memory of your loved one, there is nothing further from the truth. Life is designed to be serious, fun, and so many other contradictory things. Not having fun can bring back the person or thing you lost. Neither do you have to jump into "fun" when you aren't ready for it. However, you have to keep trying things so that you can regain your joy in life. It may not be instantaneous, but ultimately, you will get to a point when the pain becomes duller.

Living life to the fullest entails being happy. This, in turn, means that you should enjoy what you do. There is no harm in seeking activities and engaging in things you love. Take time off on days you feel sad to do new or different things. There is no need to feel guilty or ashamed about enjoying your life. Your loved one would have wanted as much or more for you.

Key Takeaways

We looked at 12 ways in which you can honor yourself and allow your grief to pass and not possess you. We looked at the following ways in particular:

- Memorializing loved ones

- Crafting your story of loss

- Setting new routines as early as possible

- Showing yourself kindness

- Taking time out to grieve

- Tackling barriers to grief

- Staying connected to others

- Taking part in community service

- Dealing with the "firsts"

- Clarifying your position concerning religion or spirituality

- Building new memories

- Having fun unapologetically

In the next chapter, we look at what resilience means, why, and how to build it.

Chapter 6:

Building Resilience in the Face of Grief

How lucky I am to have something that makes saying goodbye so hard. –A.A. Milne, Winnie-the-Pooh

Rebecca Soffer, who has turned her big loss in life into *The Modern Loss Handbook* (2022), tells us why she would rather have had no reason to write her book, pretty as it is. At the age of thirty, her mother passed away in a traumatic car accident. She had only held her mother a few hours ago, and they had been planning on meeting again for her cousin's wedding the coming weekend. Four years later, her dad died of a heart attack while he was on an international cruise. This book hadn't been her plan. She was a person who had dedicated her life to keeping her people close, eating good food, and writing and creating beautiful things that would inspire and make people laugh. However, with the double tragedies that followed quickly on the heels of one another, her life was irrevocably cleaved into "The Before" and "The After." Her grief was not just for the people she lost but also for an imagined future that was now incomplete without the people she imagined guiding her. In her own words, she felt "confused, horribly sad, sometimes angry, and even jealous" of her friends' parents, who were alive and well (Soffer, 2022, p.2).

And yet, Soffer did something with her grief that not only enabled her to come to terms with it but also created something beautiful that would inspire others—almost her initial dream itself. What she possessed was resilience in the face of grief. All of us are endowed with resilience, which can help us withstand shocks. In this part of the book, we look more closely at what it is and why it is necessary.

What Is Resilience?

Resilience, as we have already defined in the introduction to this book, is the ability to rise up after grief, loss, failure, etc. It isn't about being unaffected by things. It is instead about being affected and yet being able to go on living despite it. It isn't about "powering through" life either. The more you power through grief, the more it will catch up with you when it does. Resilience includes acceptance, acknowledgment, and even making a truce with your pain at times. However, you don't let your loss define you or your grief conquer you.

In an article I read by a psychologist who lost her 12-year-old daughter in an accident, she tells us that during her studies at the university, world-renowned psychologist and educator Martin Seligman explained that "the most common human response to adversity was not trauma, but in fact resilience" (Hone, 2020). She further tells us that this idea that resilience was innate and that we just needed to "tap into it" was very comforting during her bereavement. We also mentioned early on in this book how resilience can grow over time. Nobody has it in set quantities. However, it is possible to become more resilient with certain practices, approaches, and attitudes in life. This doesn't mean that the next time you lose something, it won't hurt. It will. However, each time something happens that you feel shouldn't have happened, you will know that you will be able to deal with it in time.

So why should you want to develop resilience?

The following are some benefits of resilience:

- **Reframing**: Resilience will help reframe the problem we experience and help us cope better with it. This means the more resilient you are, the better you will be at analyzing the situation from different perspectives.

- **Using positive emotions**: Resilience will enable you to actively use your positivity to push back against the many negative emotions that you will face. This will enable you to be more creative and productive, leaving you feeling more accomplished.

- **Being more physically and socially active**: Resilience will help you become better at embracing your body and your connection with others. This, in turn, will help you heal faster.

- **Using your unique strengths**: When you are more resilient, you will also learn the art of using the skills and strengths you possess most to solve the problems in front of you. When you are confronted with loss, one of the biggest things you initially grapple with is the number of things that you may have to wrap up or deal with. Resilience will definitely help in this regard.

- **Sense of optimism**: The biggest plus of resilience, as I see it, is that it bestows optimism, a feeling that will stay with you for life. The ability to see the good in people, places, and situations can greatly improve the quality of your life.

Now that we have looked at what it is and why you should think of developing it, we will look at the kinds of resilience and how to build it.

Types of Resilience

There are broadly four different types of resilience that one can demonstrate. These are:

- **Physical resilience**: The body's ability to recoup and recover fast, endure, or maintain its stamina and strength is called physical resilience. Physical resilience will help a person withstand ailments and other physical stressors better. It will contribute to healthy aging.

- **Emotional resilience**: Some people are better at controlling or managing their feelings, while others are flooded with them when in distress. The first will help you both physically and mentally to be in better control of yourself and resolve the issue. When emotions get in the way of clear thinking and actions, it gets harder to move ahead.

- **Psychological resilience**: This is the ability to remain calm and composed when you are faced with challenges or setbacks. This is also sometimes referred to as "mental fortitude." This ability will help combat the wear and tear associated with stress and anxiety.

- **Community resilience**: When a group of people survive calamities, natural disasters, accidents, violence, or other hardships, they build strength and hope as a unit. This is called community resilience. It is born of shared grief.

When we talk of "resilience" in the sections ahead, we are referring most to emotional and psychological resilience. Those are the kinds that will help us most in the face of grief. Of course, physical endurance is a wonderful thing too, but that would require you to train or exercise more constantly. At any rate, physical stamina without mental and emotional resilience will not work either, as any successful athlete would remind us.

How to Build Resilience

As always, it is impossible to provide an exhaustive list of ways in which you can build resilience. However, the following are some methods you can use as pointers in your quest to develop your resilience muscle:

- **Identify triggers**: This is not to avoid the triggers but to stay prepared for them. Think of the various situations in which memories of your loss could haunt you. Making a list of these triggers will enable you to find methods to overcome them or to cope with them better. They will cease to take you by surprise. If you can distinguish between the rare or one-time triggers and the continual triggers, that will also help you come up with a more concrete way of dealing with them. Just to give an example, a place nearby that you and your loved one used to frequent could be a continual trigger, whereas dealing with the arrangements for the funeral could be a one-time trigger.

- **Change the narrative**: Rumination is when you keep playing an episode or incident continuously in your mind, so much so that your thoughts keep going in a circular pattern. You can use your journal to help you think of alternatives to the story that you are telling yourself. The aim is to break the unhealthy ruminative pattern. Explore prompts like, "What if I couldn't do anything to stop what happened?" and "What happened was just meant to be." These questions will help you to break the cyclical loop of negativity that your brain is entering. The other method that you can explore is to make a list of things that you still have. This will engender a sense of gratitude for positive things that you have not lost.

- **Organize your time**: This is one of the best ways to build resilience and get things done even in the most difficult of times. Think of times in the day when you seem to have more energy. Many people find that mornings are the most productive time for them. Keep aside your chores and tasks for this time when your body and mind are most cooperative. We already talked of a to-do list, but ensure that you also segregate these tasks into priorities and non-priorities. You can do this by taking into consideration things like the urgency and importance of the tasks. For instance, conducting a funeral could be important and urgent, whereas instituting a charity in the name of the deceased may be important but not urgent. There could be things that are urgent and not important, and finally, things that are neither important nor urgent. As you tackle this to-do list, ensure you set small and achievable targets daily for yourself. Do not overdo things.

- **Embrace opportunities for self-discovery**: Think of how your grief has helped you. Right now, you may feel bogged down by the magnitude of what you have lost. However, eventually, there will also be lessons that you have learned from it, people you have gained in the process, and situations that you faced only because of your loss. These are the learning opportunities that your grief has enabled. You might also want to consider whether your loss has prompted you to appreciate life better. Not everything about losses is bad and scary, as long as you can look past the overwhelming grief that accompanies them.

- **Forgive**: It may seem hard at the moment to forgive people or situations that you feel contributed to your loss. But as a famous quote goes, "Resentment is like drinking poison and then waiting for the other person to die" (*Resentment is like...*, 2017). It will do nothing to make you feel better and will not bring any sense of closure or peace. If you want to embark on the journey of self-healing, then it is necessary to move past things that are holding you back. Anger is better than numbness, but at the end of the day, it will feed negativity into your system. We need to root out this ill will that we carry about in order to attain bliss.

- **Meditate**: Since meditation has its roots in mindfulness, it can help with not regretting the past and worrying about the future—the two thought processes that hold us back most. This activity will help you bring your mind to the present every time you feel yourself gripped by negative emotions and thoughts. Mindful eating and breathing will combat the physical stress associated with loss, while just being more rooted in your life now will help you relax and see things in perspective as part of the larger picture. While understanding that nothing can take away the impact of your loss, mindfulness and meditation will help you live with the new reality of your situation. Alluding to a famous saying, if you can't change things, then is it not best to find the strength to accept them?

- **Practice self-compassion**: Feeling lonely can be one of the worst parts of grief. We can't help but feel why we were chosen for this hardship or what we did so wrong as to warrant this punishment. Self-compassion leads to the realization that everyone suffers in their own way and that we have not been singled out for punishment. Some things to ask or say to yourself are:

  o How would you console a good friend you know who is going through the same situation as yourself?

Building this narrative will help you understand that you don't have to be so hard on yourself.

- o Put your hands on your heart as you tell yourself, "I feel this pain, but I give myself the permission to be kind to myself."

- **Develop your support network**: We spoke about this repeatedly over the previous chapters. Since it is an important part of building your innate resilience, we make a mention of it again here. This could include not just friends and family members who know what you have been through, but also colleagues from work or people at your college or university. At a time like this, you cannot be expected to work and produce results to your full potential. If your HR manager or boss understands the pressure on you, they can help relieve you at work. Your professors and other support groups on campus will help you set realistic targets for your academic work. You are not "using" your grief to "get out" of work. You are merely giving yourself a brief respite until you can catch up with yourself.

- **Face your fears**: Remember the list of triggers you identified. You can use this same list to keep exposing yourself to the same places and situations in small doses at first, perhaps, until you get more comfortable with them. For instance, keep visiting a place that triggers past memories for ten minutes at first until you can develop a tolerance for being there for hours at a stretch. This exposure therapy will help you face fears and anxieties related to a loss. Even if the anxiety doesn't completely vanish, you will be able to face it with greater courage each time you do it. It will also build resilience toward triggers in general.

- **Cultivate wellness**: Physical, emotional, and mental wellness are tantamount to recovery. Good wholesome food, drinking plenty of fluids, good quality and duration of sleep, and moderate exercise will give your body the rest it deserves. Mindfulness, consciously promoting positive thoughts, and curbing the urge to constantly criticize yourself or others will help with mental wellness. As for emotional health, forgiveness, exercise gratitude, and slow your pace. More than anything else, do not afflict more trauma on your mind and body by indulging in smoking, drinking, or using drugs. These substances may seem to dull the pain at first, but in the long run, they will only lead to worse problems for your mental and physical health.

- **Spend time in nature**: The lush, verdant greenery of trees and mountains, the chirping of the birds, sunshine, the pleasant breeze on your skin, or the rippling and gurgling of a water stream are free therapies at your disposal if you know where to find them. Many people find being at home with nature soothing, calming, and relaxing. Choose to stay away from the hustle and bustle of the city until you can regain your composure. Or, make frequent trips to areas where nature can be experienced at its best. For others who can't leave their homes as often, you can think of cultivating an indoor garden or keeping a pet, such as a dog or a cat.

- **Foster positive thoughts**: This is an active and conscious decision that you will have to make. It may not come as effortlessly as we would like it to. For instance, our first instinct may be to curse or to scream when things go wrong. With practice, you will learn to accept what it is for—something that did not happen the way you imagined it. The more you learn to see life from a larger perspective, the more you will realize that there are still things to be happy about. Like the story about the man who was complaining about the fit of his shoes until he met a person who had no legs, we often think that our problems are the worst until we see one who has had it harder than us and still seems to be coping. Don't be quick to get sucked into the negativity trap.

- **Move toward your goals**: You don't have to set yourself big, spectacular things to achieve. They can be small, mundane things you want to do, the progress of which you can measure daily or weekly. They will help your mind remain engaged and active. Break the goal into small, daily, achievable steps so that you feel a sense of self-accomplishment even on days when you feel at your lowest ebb. On some days, even crawling ahead is better than standing still. Push yourself, within reasonable limits, to what you can do and leave the rest for the next day. When you know you can do things, life becomes a lot more tolerable, and with time, you will regain your ability to take a keener interest in things.

- **Take decisive actions**: Sometimes, there are concrete things that you can do instead of just letting things happen to you passively. Don't detach from life. Where it is possible, make decisions and take action that will lead to certain outcomes. People claim that grief can jumpstart a new lease of life. However, it isn't grief but a person in grief who has to do things before they are set in motion. Be the sort of person who will not give up without resistance. Instead, shake things up by taking this as the perfect opportunity to move ahead. It may not be easy, but the results will be well worth the effort.

- **Find purpose**: Professionally or personally, find things to do that will keep you engaged and committed to the values and principles that you believe in. Without a reason in life, people often find themselves drifting aimlessly. Create the reason that you want to be alive and doing things. What you have lost should fuel your love for life even more. Think of all the things that you can do with this life that you have been blessed to live. All that you need is a purpose and motivation to keep moving ahead and to continue doing the best you can.

- **Seek help**: Remember that you aren't alone in this. There are people and support groups—personal and professional—that you can fall back on. No thought or situation is the end of the road for anyone. When life seems too much, darkness is ahead, and the going gets harder than you expected, reach out to friends, family, or your support group. Seeking psychological therapy is not failing life. It is brave to keep fighting, especially when the foe is invisible. Don't make it harder on yourself by trying to fight it all alone. Make yourself heard, and you will be amazed to see how many will step forward to help you.

Key Takeaways

- In this chapter, we looked at resilience: the ability to rise up after a fall and to keep moving ahead despite the challenges you have faced.

- Resilience will help you see life in more optimistic hues and help you tackle problems head-on, even if you are initially afraid of them.

- There are four types of resilience: physical, emotional, mental, and community resilience. Each of these is different but connected. We are looking at the development of mental and emotional resilience.

- There are various ways in which you can develop your resilient nature, such as:

  - Identifying triggering thoughts, situations, and people

  - Facing your triggers or fears

  - Changing the narrative

  - Organizing your time

  - Embracing paths to self-discovery

  - Forgiving

  - Meditating or living more mindfully

  - Practicing self-compassion

  - Developing a support network

  - Cultivating physical, emotional, and mental wellness

  - Spending time in nature

- Consciously fostering positive thoughts

- Moving toward your goals

- Finding a purpose

- Taking decisive actions

- Seeking help when you need it

In the next chapter, we look at the whole concept of "finding meaning" a little closer. Sometimes, it isn't so much as "finding" but "making" meaning of whatever life presents you with. This attitudinal shift can make all the difference between feeling helpless and feeling empowered in the face of grief.

Chapter 7:

Moving Forward and Making Meaning

April Reese tells us how, when the hospice nurse called her to tell her that her dad had passed away, the world seemed strange and half-formed to her. It was as if she was seeing everything but could not process its meaning. Even though they had been living almost 2000 miles apart, he had been a constant presence in her life from the day she was born. Outwardly, she seemed calm, doing things that were expected of her, such as letting the relatives know, tending to the governmental procedures, and informing the university where her dad had worked as a librarian for 33 years. Inside, it was a different story. She was a churning sea of anger, confusion, disbelief, despair, regret, guilt, and fear. She couldn't breathe, nor could she focus on things for long. It wasn't just the sadness but also the fear that she was going mad. It seemed she had no control over where her brain was leading her now that the primary edifice of her world was lost. It took her some research into the science of healing to understand that what she was undergoing was normal and that, with time and patience, she would be able to cope with her feelings. A line from her father's best friend finally gave her the strength that she was seeking. When we lose a friend, we experience grief along with happy memories, he wrote to her. Eventually, fond memories push the grief into the background. I'm waiting sadly but patiently" (Reese, 2021).

Often, life does not make sense, like a jigsaw puzzle that falls into place. We don't have to wait for grand things to happen for life to take on a new meaning. It can be simple, everyday things that give what we undergo a deeper meaning. Even then, we don't understand why things happen or the purpose behind them; it is merely a piecing together of the different parts of our lives into a cohesive whole. In this chapter, we look at how we can take charge of meaning-making after loss and grief.

Making Sense of Loss

Making sense of loss can be difficult because the logical part of your brain will run around in circles with questions such as *Why did I deserve this? How has my loss made my life better?* Or, *Why did I have to lose _?* You aren't going to find any answers to any of these questions. David Kessler, an expert grief counselor, wrote the book *Finding Meaning:*

The Sixth Stage of Grief (2019), is both in which he tells us his opinion about "finding" meaning after loss and grief. In a nutshell, below are some things he reiterates (Bytesco, 2022):

- Meaning is both relative and personal. Only you can make sense of your loss.

- It takes time. You may not find it until months or even years after a loss.

- It doesn't require you to understand everything. You don't need to comprehend why someone died to find meaning.

- The "why" you should answer is not why they died but why you continued to live.

- Meaning entails identifying why you live, what purpose will define the remainder of your life, and what importance you ascribe to those who are living.

- Even if you find meaning, you will never be able to equate it to the cost of losing your loved one.

- When we find meaning, we can move forward and not feel stuck in our grief.

Further, there are a series of questions that Kessler encourages us to explore as we grieve. I will only refer to some of these questions that seem most pertinent to me. However, you can check out the entire list in the book mentioned above.

- What has loss taught you?

- How would you draw comparisons between things you valued before and after your loss?

- What is important to you now?

- What is one thing you need more of in your life right now?

- How has your life changed after your loss?

- Is there something you can teach others from your experiences?

- What would you define as joy? Is there a way to increase joy in your life?

- Is there a way you think you could have prevented what happened to you?

- What inspiration can you draw from the life of your loved one? (Drake, 2022)

Now that we have looked at some questions about how you can process meaning let us look at how loss can help change you for the better, as counterintuitive as this might sound.

Personal Development Via Loss and Grief

Cheryl, who had lost her child to cancer, felt so angry and out of things. She was too tired to think ahead about a life that did not include her daughter. On most days, she felt dead inside. One day, she happened to sit in a wooded area, talking aloud to her daughter and expressing how much she missed her, wanting one last hug and kiss from her. In a while, as her grief abated, she realized how good the warmth of the sun felt on her skin. Really looking around her for the first time, she was amazed at all the life around her—the green trees, the squirrels scurrying past, and the dragonflies hovering over the little pond beside her. She finally discovered the love and compassion for all living things that she was seeking for herself. In retrospect, Cheryl found that her loss had changed what she had held to be important until then and her values. It increased her empathy for those who suffered (Janssen, 2023).

It is pretty hard to equate loss with growth or development. For most of us, loss is inextricably tied to sadness, despair, and other negative emotions. How is it possible, then, for our bodies and minds to hold the duality of positivity and negativity associated with the same stimulus? How can something be negative and positive at the same time? It seems that the statement that loss and grief can be both is not an unreasonable supposition at all. We look at the science behind this next.

Undergoing loss can help you find and establish positive changes in your life. This is not a claim that social work researchers made out of thin air (Janssen, 2023). Loss can lead to personal growth where a griever, who learns to integrate their new reality into their lives, gains new perspectives on their thoughts and feelings, a greater understanding of their hidden strengths, and new skills. In other words, they become emotionally more mature at processing their feelings and ideas, realize strengths they hadn't imagined in their previous lives, and learn to adjust to their new reality, giving them a sense of confidence and self-reliance. This type of growth stemming from loss and grief is termed "adversarial," "stress-related," or "post-traumatic" growth in science. Many people also claim that this type of growth results in closer bonds with family members and a more open mindset to understand and accept new things.

Another theory that lends weight to our argument is that the hole or vacuum created by our loss is never really filled up by other things. However, with time, there are so many experiences that we gain that the vacuum just becomes easier to carry. It is not that we fill up the hole with new things but that new things grow around the hole, which diverts our attention more than if we were to be solely focused on our loss. This is why we say that time can heal wounds and why engagement with things can speed up the healing process. However, the loss we experience lasts for a lifetime, and recovery from it cannot be rushed.

Most researchers agree on five areas in which our losses seem to have a deep and positive impact. These are:

- **Appreciation of life**: As in Cheryl's case above, grief can help in a heightened appreciation of the beauty and goodness of life. People often find more meaning in mundane situations they may have taken for granted before. Loss makes you think about how transient our lives are and how little time we have to enjoy health, happiness, peace, and other wholesome things in life. This can make life richer and more meaningful.

- **Relationships with others**: When you lose someone, you grasp how important it is to make the moments with other loved one's count. People reach out to others because they want support during their grief and also because they want to make the most of the time they have been granted on this planet. You sometimes realize the value of things better when you lose them. This will ensure that you spend more time with the people who really matter to you. This, in turn, increases the significance of your life.

- **New possibilities in life**: As the adage goes, "When a door closes, a new one opens." It sometimes takes a loss for us to realize new opportunities in life that have been staring us in the face all along. The classic example is people who are laid off or lose their jobs to find new professions where there is more scope for personal fulfillment. These people sometimes also tell us that had they not been laid off, perhaps they would have continued in their old jobs hear-heartedly and possibly even miserably unhappy.

- **Personal strength**: When you live with a person who takes care of half your household or other responsibilities, you don't even have to bother about those things. When you lose them, you suddenly have to step into these new responsibilities or caregiving roles—perhaps things you did not even know you could do before. This is when you rely on your personal strengths and recognize qualities that you possess but are dormant. Using these newfound strengths can often seem liberating and will help you tackle the pain of grief as well.

- **Spiritual change**: We have mentioned this before. It needn't be that you suddenly find God or religion, though that does often happen to many people after a loss. However, any kind of loss will make you ponder more about the meaning and purpose of your life and how you can find personal fulfillment while also being of service to others. This reflection will help you lead a life more aligned with the deeper sense of satisfaction you want out of life. You will find ways and means to make your words and actions count.

We have looked at how loss and grief can bring positive growth in our lives, even though we may find it hard to accept at first that something so terrible can benefit us. In the next section, we look at what a growth mindset means and how we can incorporate it into our post-loss coping mechanisms.

Growth Mindset as a Coping Strategy

The Japanese don't throw away broken ceramic containers. They fuse the broken pieces together with a certain kind of gum dusted with powdered gold. The fracture lines on such repaired items can be seen clearly in gold as the vessel becomes usable again. This art is called Kintsugi. It is a perfect metaphor for why broken items should not be disposed of. In fact, they can be more beautiful and stronger than ever before. Similarly, our grief need not destroy or weaken us, as it is popularly thought. We can piece together our lives to find greater strength and meaning, should we choose to do so. The keyword here is "choosing" because without our consent, moving on is impossible. We need to permit ourselves to walk through and overcome our grief to rebuild our lives. We will also need to be more proactive in allowing new experiences, memories, and situations to shape our lives. This is what will add beauty and purpose to our lives.

If you look at what we are doing here, it is not very different from what we call developing a "growth mindset," though the term may conjure up images of business and career development classes more than those related to grief management or counseling.

A growth mindset refers to our ability to believe that our skills, perceptions, and feelings are ever-evolving and that we can change, modify, or improve upon them as and when the need arises. There are primarily three aspects that contribute to one's growth mindset (Collins, n.d.):

- **Self-efficacy**: This is the belief that you can do things efficiently and well. For instance, you know that you can get things done, see a process through to its completion, or handle the finance and logistics of a program or event. These contribute to the idea that "I can do it." The more such things you learn to do, even as you navigate your grief, the better your sense of self-efficacy will be. You will also understand that you don't need anybody else to complete you or do things for you. You are enough. That in itself will give you a lot of peace.

- **Self-esteem**: This is tied up to who you are, your sense of identity, and what you expect from others. Questions you can ask yourself include: *Am I worthy of love? Do I deserve respect? Do I inspire others?* Answers to these questions will reveal whether you need to improve your self-esteem. What it means for managing grief is that you should feel entitled to live life fully again. You don't shun or isolate yourself owing to your loss but rather seek new ways of living, thinking, and feeling. Empowering yourself to be loved and cared for is about self-esteem, and it can provide growth during grief.

- **Self-management**: When you know that you are capable of tending to your work, emotions, and thoughts, that is self-management. All the self-care practices we covered in Chapters 4 and 5 that help you cope with your grief are examples of how you choose to manage yourself physically, emotionally, mentally, and spiritually in the wake of your loss.

Some other additional ways in which you can decide to embrace a growth mindset are (Pisello, 2022):

- **Accepting challenges**: Every setback you face is an exciting opportunity to showcase your unique problem-solving abilities. When you look at challenges during grief this way, you will see a huge difference in how you respond to situations.

- **Getting outside your comfort zone**: When you suffer a loss, you want to make life as cushy and cozy as you can. This is a great survival tactic initially. However, in the long term, if you continue to make things easy for yourself, then you are making yourself fragile. Every new thing will throw you into a panic or flutter. Instead, slowly, you have to put yourself in situations you would rather not. The more you do it, the easier it gets.

- **Maintaining an optimistic attitude**: This one is easier said than done. I know silver linings can be hard to find when the clouds are as heavy and dark as yours. However, this is also a practice you can train yourself in. The more you instruct your brain to look out for the positives in situations, the more your mind will naturally gravitate toward happiness and brightness. An optimistic attitude will improve your mental and physical well-being.

- **Working**: This is another great tactic for developing a growth mindset. When you keep working toward your goals, you are, at least for that time, keeping aside your pain. This, of course, can go to the extreme, where people throw themselves into their work to avoid their grief, which can be just as harmful as wallowing in it. With work, it is essential to find the ideal balance so that you continue to be productive but don't overwork yourself into anxiety.

- **Serving others**: This is one of the best ways in which you can develop a growth mindset. When you know that your actions and words can impact people around you and make positive changes in their lives, you feel gratified. There is no greater satisfaction than knowing that your work is helping other people.

In other words, when you stop asking "Why me?" and start asking "What next?" is the pinnacle of adopting a growth mindset. In the last section of this chapter, we look at why embracing vulnerability is as important for your healing journey as it is for living a life of better quality.

Embracing Vulnerability

Brene Brown narrates an anecdote of how she was invited as a speaker, and the host wanted to introduce her as a "storyteller" because they felt it would rope in a bigger crowd than if they called her a "researcher," a person who was usually associated with boring lectures. Brown was conflicted because the researcher felt that being called a storyteller would undermine her work. Finally, she accepted it with a shrug, thinking of her qualitative research, based on human stories, as "data with a soul."

In her famous TEDx Talk (Brown, 2010), she talks about how hard it was for her to come to terms with the beauty of vulnerability. She went about collecting stories from people about human connection over the six-and-a-half years it took for her to complete her PhD in social work. Over this time, she had many stories, and yet she did not understand how to process all of this data into a theory so that she could explain the messiness of human experience.

Brown further describes her struggle with trying to categorize the human experience and what one could make of it. One thing she discovered was that human resilience, happiness, and progress were tied to a certain quality in people, which made them more courageous and compassionate and allowed them to connect to people better. She kept prodding further about what this elusive thing was that set apart some people from others and allowed the former to live life "king-sized." Finally, she understood that what made them different was the fact that they did not fight but rather embraced vulnerability.

Vulnerability is not comfortable because it entails taking a degree of emotional risk without knowing the consequences. For instance, in a relationship, people wait for the other to say, "I love you," first because they are scared that if they do it and then the other doesn't reciprocate, they will get hurt. This fear of taking a leap of faith is what holds many people back from leading a fuller life.

In grief as well, embracing vulnerability can bring back all the positive emotions such as joy, love, empathy, and belonging. Thus, instead of trying to suppress vulnerability, as we are often instructed or tempted to do, we must acknowledge and walk into vulnerability. When we try to beat back vulnerability, we also often numb the other good emotions we just talked about above.

Lastly, many of us erroneously feel that our goal in life is to make uncertain things certain by giving shape, meaning, and purpose to them or by analyzing why they happen. But sometimes, it is just better to leave things as they are. Nature is beautiful because there is a sense of mystery to it, even for those who diligently study the science behind it. Similarly, perhaps instead of trying to find meaning in our loss, it could be more productive to accept it just as it is and to contemplate ways of making it meaningful through purposeful thoughts and actions. Meaning-making is often more in our hands than in that of the cosmos, universe, or God.

Key Takeaways

We talked about various ways in which we find meaning in the loss and grief that we have suffered:

- There are questions, vetted by experts, we can ask ourselves that would bring more clarity to us during this meaning-making process.

- Grief and loss are not all bad. They often lead to personal development if one keeps an open mind.

- It is possible to promote a growth mindset as you grieve so that your loss leads to you gaining some insight into life and its purpose. But this requires work.

- Finally, embracing vulnerability through the process of grieving will bring back the joy, empathy, belongingness, and love that we often seek during that period.

In the next and last chapter of this book, we look at how we can use what we have learned thus far to help others in their grieving journey. Remember, teaching is often the most powerful way of learning and relearning too.

Chapter 8:

Supporting Others in Grief

Deep grief sometimes is almost like a specific location, a coordinate on a map of time. When you are standing in that forest of sorrow, you cannot imagine that you could ever find your way to a better place. But if someone can assure you that they themselves have stood in that same place, and now have moved on, sometimes this will bring hope. – Elizabeth Gilbert

Amy Hoggart (2018) tells us of her harrowing experience when her father died of cancer. He was only in his 60s and was in terrible pain. Her mother and dad were going away on a short vacation, and she knew that they would be miserable. Her father would be uncomfortable and tired, and her mother was too caught up in his needs to really enjoy herself. Though she tried to hold up as best as she could, some days were difficult. She couldn't bear to see her dad literally dying a little each day and suffering so much. When she couldn't bear it, she opened up to one of her dear friends. She told them the honest truth: Her father was getting sicker, that the National Health Service (NHS) might not cover another treatment, and that he was growing more depressed by the day.

Her friend wanted to focus more on the vacation and told her how happy they were that her parents were finally going on a short trip. Amy felt unheard and unable to be fully honest anymore in the face of what seemed like the friend's persistence in ignoring the harder bits of what she was trying to convey. She also had well-meaning family members and friends who would try to compare her dad's situation with pets or other older relatives they had lost. This would again make Amy angry because it didn't seem fair to be comparing her dad to someone's pet or to a distant relative in their 90s.

You must have faced similar situations, too. Many of these people, trying to console you, are at a loss for how to talk to a person who is grieving. While they mean to offer their hope and sympathy, at the end of the day, the things they say come across as inappropriate, condescending, or even flippant. It leaves you feeling angry, neglected, upset, or irritated.

In this chapter, we look at conscious ways in which we can offer our help and support to those who are grieving by acknowledging their grief and not belittling it. We will be drawing from all the strategies that we have discussed in the earlier chapters to focus on how we can alleviate the pain of others by being present for them and listening to them. Often, there is not much more that we can do, and neither do these people expect otherwise from you. Here, we also look at how our own experiences can be used to provide sustenance to those who are at a place you were only a while ago.

Some Challenges of Supporting Others in Grief

As a person who has withstood the travails of grief and sorrow, offering help to others in the same situation will come with its own set of challenges. On the one hand, as a person who has undergone a similar situation, you may be more attuned to the nuances of another's grief and loss. You may also be naturally more empathetic to their problems. However, you could also find a resurgence of your own grief through their loss. You could find yourself being dragged back into the pit of negative and dark emotions, thoughts, and memories. Let us look at some particular challenges that offering help to the grieving from the fountain of your experience could bring about.

- **Feeling vulnerable**: When you listen to another person's recital of troubles that are very similar to the one you underwent, a part of you will feel lighter or relieved because you are no longer alone. Here is someone who knows exactly what you went through. You feel that sharing your side of the story is natural and will help you both cope with your respective losses. However, another part of you could be traumatized because you are reliving your grief. Just when you thought that you could move on and find a semblance of normalcy in your life again, everything is getting disrupted because you feel obligated to be pulled back into your suffering with the person you are trying to help. This can seem contradictory, and you might be pulled at once by the opposing desires of wanting to help and withdrawing from this other person.

- **Maintaining boundaries**: Maintaining a healthy boundary with a person who is grieving is essential for our health and well-being. Yet, this might seem selfish to many. People who want to offer their support neglect to create a safe mental, physical, and emotional boundary for themselves. As a result, they end up pouring themselves into helping others without taking care of themselves. Eventually, this "sacrifice" takes an emotional, physical, and mental toll on them. They become depressed and unable to help the people they want to. One of the first things that you have to do, should you choose to help another in grief, is to draw up certain healthy boundaries so that you are in control of your health and safety. Unless these are in place, you will do more damage to the person you mean to help.

- **Self-care while sharing grief**: When you mean to offer your support to a person who is grieving, you need to put a self-care routine for yourself in place. This could include measures to improve and maintain your physical, mental, emotional, and spiritual wellness. Engage in exercise, hobbies, and pleasurable activities, and talk to people who keep you happy. Helping another doesn't mean that you put your life on hold. When a flight hits turbulence, you have to put on your oxygen mask before you venture out to help others put on theirs. Similarly, if you aren't happy, you can't make another person happy. It is as simple as that.

Now that we have looked at what the challenges of providing help could be let us look at effective strategies—both dos and don'ts—for dealing with another's grief.

Communicating With Empathy

Empathy is putting yourself in the other person's shoes and helping them as you would want to be helped if you were them. It is not an easy thing to do because, as human beings, we are wired to be selfish. Our sense of self-preservation usually prevails over all other considerations. Therefore, communicate with empathy with someone who is grieving. You need to be sensitive to their needs.

Many times, as you may have discovered from your own experience, people who grieve do not require platitudes and reasons for what happened. Instead, they need you to be present and to listen to their problems, fears, and anxieties. They are not asking you to resolve anything but simply want to vent and feel their thoughts and emotions validated.

Empathetic communication, which includes a large share of listening to others with an open, non-judgmental mindset, can help the grieving person to express themselves, which is the way to healing. It also means that you do not deprecate, ignore, or gloss over the hard parts of their narrative. The following are some dos and don'ts of the process.

Dos

- **Reach out**: When you hear of a grieving person, you are often confused about what to say. This confusion and awkwardness you feel over how to react manifests as dilly-dallying over the question of how to reach out. Therefore, you postpone a decision on it. Instead, think of how you would like people to have reached out when you were grieving. It doesn't have to be a profound quote or words of wisdom. You can simply call up and say hi. Be direct in saying that you heard the news and would like to see if there is anything you can do to help them. Make it clear that you are available and willing to be of service should they need you.

- **Gauge their reaction**: Don't be quick to impose your decisions where they aren't welcome. After having offered to help, allow the other person to speak. Sometimes, we are so solicitous that we forget to really understand what the other person needs. People who come to the console sometimes keep talking about the dead person, failing to notice that it is only making things worse for the grieving person. When you do want to help, let it be in a way that puts the other person at ease. In short, their needs come first. You are not here to be seen doing your duty by helping them. You are here to help them the way they want to be helped.

- **Listen**: This is the golden rule of empathy, after all. Listen to what they are saying. Listen to their needs. Listen if they want to speak of their loss. Don't force them to talk, but be present when they show signs of wanting to. This also includes following their body language. Sometimes, their gestures and expressions convey more than what they are saying. Remember how words often fail us in moments of emotional and mental upheaval? Listen to your instincts when showing empathy for them. Sometimes, it is okay to lean in and offer a hug, while others may not appreciate that kind of physical proximity.

- **Express love, not always in words**: You may know the person grieving well before their loss. Remember that they are the same person fundamentally, even after their loss. Think of ways other than words to express your love. If you think they may be fine with it, go ahead and bake a batch of cookies for them. Squeeze their hand in sympathy, hug them, or kiss them if you feel they need it. This does not mean you force yourselves upon them, but you can use your gut instinct to console them. It is nice to use WhatsApp or message them to ask them how they are doing. (Though I will not recommend this for the first contact you establish with them after their loss.) You can send them flowers to remind them that you are thinking of them, or books if they are the reading kind.

- **Ask how they feel**: When you talk to them, ask them how they feel. Of course, not everyone may be articulate enough to explain the whole gamut of emotions they are going through.

However, just the fact that you care about how they feel will make it easier for them to talk. If and when they are willing to talk, follow up with genuine questions about the things that they are saying. This will make them feel heard. If they aren't ready to talk about certain things, don't push them, but let them know that you are here for them whenever they may need you.

- **Acknowledge the pain**: Be kind and accepting of their pain. You can't expect them to diminish their suffering just to make you feel comfortable or at ease with the situation. This is their day, not yours. All you need to tell them is that you understand how tough it is and that you are listening. Do not ask them to be grateful for the things that did not go wrong. Do not even think, much less say things like, "It could have been worse." Follow the maxim that tells us that if we can't say anything good, then it is better to be silent.

- **Be sensitive**: In things you say and do, be sensitive. Do not assume things; ask them if it is alright for you to help them in a certain way. Be spontaneous and gentle. They don't expect you to offer words of profound wisdom or help them make sense of the tragedy. All they want is your presence and whatever help you can offer at this time. Don't overwhelm them immediately with questions about the future or "what next?" Let them grieve what they have lost. There is time to consider the implications later when time takes the edge off their grief.

- **Sit in silence**: There could be people who aren't yet ready to talk. Don't assume that they expect you to fill the silence with blustering small talk, condolences, or words about the departed, etc. At times, you can just sit with them in the silence of their loss. Your presence will make them feel less alone in their grief, even if you don't talk volubly about it. Use your intuition to decide when it would be a good time to break the silence, how to keep your message, and how to offer help in such cases.

- **Be prepared for mood swings**: As you know from your own experience, grief ebbs and flows for a while. The whole cycle could repeat itself continuously. This can leave a person angry, irritated, and sad by turns. Just because a certain time has elapsed since their loss, you can't expect them to perk up and put everything behind them. Allow them to work through their emotions. These mood swings are not permanent. They will pass as they learn to accept their loss and grief. Don't push them away simply because they are a little erratic at the moment. This could be when they need you most.

- **Stay connected**: If you mean to help, then you may have to stick around for a while. If that's not possible physically, make an effort to stay in touch via calls or messages. Just keep it simple by telling them that you were thinking of them or if there is something you can do to help. Remember, grieving could be new for them, and they may be embarrassed to disturb people by asking for help. When you proactively offer your service, you are taking the burden of asking for help off their shoulders.

- **Offer practical help**: Think of the routine things that a grieving person may be too overwhelmed to do on their own right now. This could include picking kids up from school, doing the dishes or laundry, or cooking. Offering to run errands for them or pick up groceries from the store, etc., are some practical ways in which you can help around the house. Funeral arrangements are an area where the person might need some assistance immediately. You don't have to take on everything, of course, but chip in where you can.

Don'ts

- **Keep waiting**: Don't unnecessarily delay asking a person if they want help. Remember that the earlier you talk to them, the better for them and for you. When you keep postponing the moment, not only will the whole interaction become harder, but it will also give the feeling that you don't really care for the person or their situation. For instance, Amy Hoggart (2018) tells us how her mother received a letter from a relative saying how sorry they were about her dad's illness the day he died. Her dad had been ailing for three whole years, and to her, it was just ridiculous that they sent that letter so late in the day.

- **Be dramatic**: If you want to help, let it stem from a genuine impulse to help the person grieving. Do not try to dig into details about things they don't want to discuss. Most of all, do not use their vulnerability to gather information for yourself or other gossip mongers. Keep your words and actions kind, authentic, and consistent every day. Do not try to make a statement about how much you care, especially when you aren't very close to the person. At this point, let the griever's terms govern interactions rather than yours.

- **Only focus on the good**: You may have the best intentions at heart in wanting to steer the conversation to the good times and memories. Every time the person grieving wants to talk about difficult or hard issues, you try to make it "less distressing" by harping on the positives. However, this does not really help that person. They want to vent their grief and perhaps talk about it in all its complexity while you are determinedly negating a chance for them to do this. They will feel unheard and think that you are trying to invalidate their emotions. This will eventually make them shut themselves off from you.

- **Put an optimistic spin on everything**: A continuation of the previous point, do not try to console people by saying that not all is bad or that things could have been worse. That is not what they want to hear right now. You might want to tell them how loved and full the life of the deceased was, but for them, perhaps there was more that the person could have seen, achieved, or spent more time with. Let them grieve what they have lost without you trying to turn it around into a positive experience.

- **Make comparisons**: Refrain from comparing somebody's loss with yours or that of other people you know. Everyone grieves in their own way, and you really can't know how much the thing or person they lost costs them. Grief and loss are not quantifiable or comparable. Though you are trying to tell them that there are others like them, it might be better to hold your tongue just for now. Later, if they ask you for help in contacting support groups, you can tell them about others who have faced losses like theirs and worked through it.

- **Undervalue or trivialize their pain**: This is a strict no. You may think that giving too much attention to their sorrow will not help them heal. Therefore, you try to construct narratives that might help them see why they had to lose their loved one. The fact is that, in most cases, this does not help. Some statements not to make in the face of another's grief are:

    - "Your loved one is in a better place:" Nobody really knows this for sure. Heaven is still only a belief, no matter how strong that faith is.

    - "It is God's will:" Maybe the person grieving does not really believe in God or religion.

    - "At least they are no longer suffering:" We don't know that the person who died would rather have died than take the pain.

- **Give advice**: Avoid all statements that begin with, "You should...," "You ought to...," or "Have you considered..." It is too soon for the person grieving to have thought elaborately about anything. Chances are they are still exhausted, sad, angry, and confused about what has happened. They don't want your counseling right now. All they want is an outlet for their grief and pain.

- **Avoid them**: This would seem obvious but do not cross the street or pretend to be busy on your phone because you don't want to talk to somebody who is in grief. You may think that you are saving them from an embarrassing discussion or try to tell yourself that you are giving them "space." In reality, it is rude, insensitive, and hurtful. You must offer to help and then leave it to them to take you up on your offer. Though there is no need to keep forcing yourself upon them, there is also no need to run away from them.

- **Offer religious or spiritual platitudes**: We have mentioned a few already, but just to reiterate, faith is a very personal matter and not something to be thrust upon another. If you believe in a higher presence, that is great, and it can be a wonderful source of solace. But not everyone may share the same idea. Unless you know for a fact that the grieving person is a believer, do not offer consolatory remarks related to "God's will" or that "it was for the best," etc.

- **Comment on their appearance**: Grieving people could look alright on the outside and still be deeply sorrowful. They might lose weight and hair and look tired if they don't get enough sleep. Do not make any comments on their appearance. In short, don't say anything that might make them feel bad about their lack of obvious grieving or about the plainly visible part of their sorrow.

In the last section of the chapter, we list a few resources that could guide you or anyone you know through grief and loss.

Some Resources That May Help

The following are some resources, referenced at the end of this book, that you could consider for yourself or anybody else struggling to cope with the pangs of grief. You will find a plethora of material online by doing a Google search. However, be sure to cross-check the relevance, authenticity, and accuracy of the content you may come across.

Books

- *The Comfort Book* (2022) by Matt Haig

- Atlas of the Heart: Mapping Meaningful Connection and the Language of Human Experience (2021) by Brené Brown

- Surviving the Holidays Without You: Navigating Grief During Special Seasons (2019) by Gary Roe

- *The Other Side of Sadness* (2019) by George A. Bonanno, PhD

- Non-Death Loss and Grief: Context and Clinical Implications (2019), edited by Darcy L. Harris

- It's OK That You're Not OK: Meeting Grief and Loss in a Culture That Doesn't Understand (2017) by Megan Devine

- Bearing the Unbearable: Love, Loss, and the Heartbreaking Path of Grief (2017) by Dr. Joanne Cacciatore and Jeffrey Rubin

Websites and Videos

- The American Foundation for Suicide Prevention (website)

- Grief and Loss Resources on American Counseling Association (website)

- *Grief is Good* - TED Talk by Joe Primo (video)

- We don't "move on" from grief. We move forward with it, TED Talk by Nora McInerny (video)

- Grieving.com (website)

- Association for Death Education and Counseling (website)

Places to Contact

Some of the following places may have grief support networks or systems in place.

- Hospices

- Hospitals

- Funeral homes

- Counseling Centers in colleges and universities

- Religious centers or places of worship

The most important fact to keep in mind while helping someone journey through their grief is to stay kind, open, and sincere.

Key Takeaways

In this chapter, we focused on how to help others who may be going through similar loss and grief cycles by:

- identifying the main challenges associated with offering help and support.

- understanding the dos and don'ts of communicating with kindness and empathy.

- being aware of some resources for navigating loss, grief, and hope.

Conclusion

Grief is not a disorder, a disease or a sign of weakness. It is an emotional, physical and spiritual necessity, the price you pay for love. The only cure for grief is to grieve. –Earl Grollman

Since all the stories that we shared throughout the course of this book are related to dying or death, let me wrap up with a few stories on non-death losses, which can be as sad as a person close to you passing on. Take the pandemic for example. Everyone reading this book might have felt a certain anxiety related to everything surrounding it. Some of us lost family and friends, jobs, the security of our daily routines, and even the plans we had for the future. And yet, some of this discomfort that we felt was not all anxiety. More than one psychotherapist, including Joe Pinsker, David Kessler, and Lori Gottlieb, has attested to the fact that what we felt was grief. We felt the loss of our daily life, safety, connections, normal life, and small celebrations of life such as missed birthday parties, sports matches, and holidays, as we weren't able to do the things we had always taken for granted (Richardson & Millar, 2022).

Another poignant article in *The New York Times* by Zoe Fowler (2023) sums up what loss can feel, like even when it isn't about death. She talks of her 25-year-old divorce from her husband and then about how she managed to slowly give away and declutter the remnants of their life together. When her husband returned from rehab a few years ago, he decided that he no longer wanted to live with his wife in their home, where they had raised their two grown daughters. She had not been able to afford their large house and had moved to a smaller unit while putting away the majority of the things they possessed in a storage locker. The things would have remained there had she not read of Swedish death cleaning, which apparently allowed people to live lighter if they decluttered the things they owned. Determined to "live lighter," she opened the storage locker and gave away a lot of things she did not want to see again, much less use because of the sadness she felt associated with the memories they held for her. Her biggest donation was her wedding shoes, which she presented to her younger daughter, for whom they were a perfect fit. Other things she saved were the wooden cot, which bore the teeth marks of her daughters from when they were teething, and an orange-stuffed dog with mismatched eyes that her grandmother had repaired for her. Her biggest fear remains that she will lose not just her husband but also the memories of things that were once so precious to her.

To recap, *Coping With Loss* covers in eight giant steps what one can do in the face of loss and debilitating sadness that refuses to let go of you. They are:

1. **Understanding why and how your mind and body grieve**: We looked at the ways in which grief can be formed and manifest itself. We also explored how ignoring grief can cause prolonged or complicated grief. Though there are clinically defined durations for how long healthy grief should last, these are more descriptive than prescriptive. Neither science nor the people around you can define how long you should grieve.

2. **The five stages of grieving and how myths related to loss are merely that**: The five stages of grief are merely a touchstone for you to understand your grief and its emotions better. Hardly anybody moves precisely from each of those stages to the next. More often than not, grief is a cyclical process where you will find yourself moving back and forth between the stages. Each person, having experienced their grief differently, will give you advice on what you ought to do. However, these do not work. You are you, and your grief is yours to deal with in a manner that serves you.

3. Communicating loss with a personal circle of people who care about you and identifying when you may need professional help in healing from grief: Ask yourself with whom and how much of your story you want to share. Sharing is a great way to not have to carry the burden all by yourself. If you prefer anonymity and more impersonal intervention, then professional therapy might be the route you are seeking.

4. **Exploring emotional outlets such as journaling, mindfulness, and creative arts**: Journaling helps create a word picture of your loved one and captures your feelings at their most difficult phase. Mindfulness and meditation are strategies that will help you untangle your complex thoughts and find clarity in the present moment. Creative expression allows you to choose from several media and materials to express your grief in a manner that makes the most sense to you.

5. **Try out the 12 ways in which you can honor yourself and the memory of your loss**: These will help you take care of your health and mental peace while shattering the barriers to healthy grieving.

6. **Building and using emotional and psychological resilience so that your grief becomes more bearable**: This step includes several practices that you can start, which will aid in personalizing your grief as you become more immune to it.

7. Moving from finding to making meaning of your loss by actively adopting personal development, a growth mindset, and embracing vulnerability: While science has established how grief can improve your quality of life, a growth mindset will make this process more practically achievable. Running toward vulnerability and accepting it as that which makes us more human is essential to healing and living a better life.

8. Identifying challenges in supporting other grieving people and overcoming those via good communication laced with plenty of empathy and kindness: In short, treat another person who grieves as you would want to be treated when you are undergoing your own.

Ultimately, we can only reiterate what we know to be a fact. Grief is not a competition, and there is no one right way of doing it. You have to find your way through its murky depths. Fear not; there is definitely a way out and a way forward. Just keep looking and moving ahead.

I hope that this book has provided you with a little strength and respite in your darkest times. If it has made even a modicum of difference in the way you perceive life, I hope you will share and recommend this resource to others like you who may benefit from reading it. If you have enjoyed this book, please don't forget to leave an honest review for it. I love feedback, constructive criticism, and discussions on the subjects of loss and grief. I would like to hear from you about your personal tussles and triumphs on your healing journey.

I wish each one of you the very best in your paths ahead. May you find love, laughter, and, above all else, a new lease of life!

Maria Holden

About the Author

Maria Holden is a passionate advocate for healing and personal growth. With an empathetic heart and a keen understanding of the human spirit, she crafts transformative narratives that have touched the lives of countless readers worldwide. Born with an innate curiosity about the human psyche, she invites readers on profound introspective journeys, emphasizing the power of self-compassion and empathy. Maria's writing continues to be a beacon of hope, reminding us of all the transformative power of kindness and understanding.

References

American Counseling Association. (2019). *Grief and loss.* Counseling.org. https://www.counseling.org/knowledge-center/mental-health-resources/grief-and-loss-resources

American Foundation for Suicide Prevention. (2019, February 28). AFSP. https://afsp.org/

Association for death education and counseling. (2019). Adec.org. https://www.adec.org/

Brown, B., & TEDx Talks. (2010). *The power of vulnerability* [Video]. YouTube. https://www.youtube.com/watch?v=X4Qm9cGRub0

Bytesco. (2022, June 28). *Finding meaning in grief.* Samaritans. https://samaritanshope.org/blog/finding-meaning-in-grief/#:~:text=Finding%20that

Cherry, K. (2023, November 9). *What is art therapy?* Verywell Mind. https://www.verywellmind.com/what-is-art-therapy-2795755#:~:text=The%20creation%20or%20appreciation%20of

Collins, B. (n.d.). *Cultivating a growth mindset when working with grieving students.* Heinemann Blog. Retrieved November 22, 2023, from https://blog.heinemann.com/cultivating-a-growth-mindset-when-working-with-grieving-students

Cruse. (n.d.). *Understanding the five stages of grief.* Cruse Bereavement Support. https://www.cruse.org.uk/understanding-grief/effects-of-grief/five-stages-of-grief/#:~:text=The%20five%20stages%20%E2%80%93%20denial%2C%20anger

Dealing with grief - one woman's personal story of grief and loss. (n.d.). GriefAndSympathy. https://www.griefandsympathy.com/dealing-with-grief.html

Drake, A. E. (2022, January 3). *Finding meaning from grief.* Full Circle. https://fullcirclegc.org/2022/01/03/finding-meaning-from-grief/

Fowler, Z. (2023, November 24). First my husband left, then my stuff. *The New York Times.* https://www.nytimes.com/2023/11/24/style/modern-love-my-husband-left-first-then-my-stuff.html?smid=url-share

Help for Coping with Loss. (n.d.). Grieving.com. https://forums.grieving.com/

Hoggart, A. (2018, January 26). *21 ways to help someone you love through grief.* Time; Time. https://time.com/5118994/advice-for-helping-grieving-friend/

Hone, L. (2020, February 19). *What I learned about resilience in the midst of grief.* Greater Good. https://greatergood.berkeley.edu/article/item/what_i_learned_about_resilience_in_the_midst_of_grief

Janssen, S. (2023). Growth during grief. *Social Work Today*, 14. https://www.socialworktoday.com/archive/Summer23p14.shtml

Mahajan, S. (n.d.). *A mother's story of overcoming grief.* Live Love Laugh. Retrieved November 12, 2023, from https://www.thelivelovelaughfoundation.org/blog/self-care-support/a-mother-s-story-of-overcoming-grief

McInerny, N., & TED. (2019). *We don't "move on" from grief. We move forward with it* [Video]. YouTube. https://www.youtube.com/watch?v=khkJkR-ipfw

Monica. (2020, October 23). *Grief: My personal story.* The Mix. https://www.themix.org.uk/mental-health/looking-after-yourself/grief-my-personal-story-38141.html#:~:text=I%20remember%20that%20instead%20of

Morris, S. (2017). *An introduction to coping with grief.* In Internet Archive. London Robinson. https://archive.org/details/introductiontoco0000morr_i3r1/page/76/mode/1up

Mukherjee, C. (2022, July 6). *What is catharsis and how does it help in emotional release?* The Pleasant Mind. https://thepleasantmind.com/catharsis/#:~:text=Catharsis%20is%20an%20emotional%20release

Nigella Lawson quote. (n.d.). Quotefancy. Retrieved October 31, 2023, from https://quotefancy.com/quote/1289028/Nigella-Lawson-You-don-t-go-around-grieving-all-the-time-but-the-grief-is-still-there-and

Non-Death loss and grief: Context and clinical implications. (2019). In D. L. Harris (Ed.), Amazon (1st edition). Routledge. https://www.amazon.com/Non-Death-Grief-Death-Dying-Bereavement/dp/113832082X

Penrose, K. (2021, February 11). *10 touching stories about love and death just in time for Valentine's day.* FuneralOne Blog. https://blog.funeralone.com/holidays/love-stories/

Pisello, T. (2022, April 8). *GROWTH: A mindset for healing.* Growth through Grief. https://growththroughgrief.org/growth-implementing-a-mindset-for-healing-and-actualization/

Primo, J. & TEDx. (2017). *Grief is good* [Video]. YouTube. https://www.youtube.com/watch?v=snbc6jg0Oro

Quotes about grief. (2021, July 22). Psych Central. https://psychcentral.com/addictions/quotes-about-grief#quotes

Quotes: Earl Grollman. (n.d.). My Grief Assist. https://www.mygriefassist.com.au/inspiration-

resources/quotes/#:~:text=%22Grief%20is%20itself%20a%2
0medicine.%22&text=%22Memory%20is%20a%20way%20of

A quote from Elizabeth Gilbert. (n.d.). Goodreads. Retrieved November 23, 2023, from https://www.goodreads.com/quotes/288693-deep-grief-sometimes-is-almost-like-a-specific-location-a

Resentment is like taking poison and waiting for the other person to die. (2017, August 19). Quote Investigator. https://quoteinvestigator.com/2017/08/19/resentment/

Richardson, L., & Millar, B. (2022). Grief and the non-death losses of Covid-19. *Phenomenology and the Cognitive Sciences.* https://doi.org/10.1007/s11097-022-09878-8

Rusch, H. L., Rosario, M., Levison, L. M., Olivera, A., Livingston, W. S., Wu, T., & Gill, J. M. (2019). The effect of mindfulness meditation on sleep quality: a systematic review and meta-analysis of randomized controlled trials. *Annals of the New York Academy of Sciences, 1445*(1), 5–16. https://doi.org/10.1111/nyas.13996

Servaty-Seib, & Lynn, H. (2015). *We get it: voices of grieving college students and young adults.* Jessica Kingsley Publishers. Internet Archive. https://archive.org/details/wegetitvoicesofg0000serv/page/28/mode/1up?view=theater

Smith, M., Robinson, L., & Segal, J. (2019). *Coping with Grief and Loss.* HelpGuide.org. https://www.helpguide.org/articles/grief/coping-with-grief-and-loss.htm

Soffer, R. (2022). The modern loss handbook: An interactive guide to moving through grief and building your resilience. Running Press Adult. *Amazon.* https://www.amazon.in/Modern-Loss-Handbook-Interactive-Resilience/dp/0762474815?asin=0762474815&revisionId=&format=4&depth=1

Sreenivas, S. (2021, August 3). *What is grief counseling?* WebMD. https://www.webmd.com/balance/grief-counseling

10 Inspirational quotes about overcoming grief. (2022, September 26). Southern Metropolitan Cemeteries Trust. https://smct.org.au/blog/10-inspirational-quotes-about-overcoming-grief

10 quotes that beautifully express what grief feels like. (n.d.). Hospiscare. Retrieved November 18, 2023, from https://www.hospiscare.co.uk/how-we-help/advice-support/information-about-grief/10-quotes-that-beautifully-express-what-grief-feels-like/#:~:text=In%20time%2C%20it%20can%20recede

What is grief? Cleveland Clinic. (2023, February 22). Cleveland Clinic. https://my.clevelandclinic.org/health/diseases/24787-grief